Genesis and Semitic tradition

John D. Davis, John D. Davis Ph. D.

BIBLIOLIFE

GENESIS

AND

SEMITIC TRADITION

BY

JOHN D. DAVIS, Ph.D.

PROFESSOR OF SEMITIC PHILOLOGY AND OLD TESTAMENT HISTORY IN THE
THEOLOGICAL SEMINARY AT PRINCETON, N. J.

NEW YORK

CHARLES SCRIBNER'S SONS

1894

PREFACE

BABYLONIAN traditions concerning primitive times were cited by Greek and Jewish writers. These reports indicated that the peoples of Semitic race or Babylonian culture who dwelt on the Tigris and Euphrates rivers had accounts of the early ages which told the same story as the Hebrew narratives or showed common conceptions with them. But the genuineness, at times, and the antiquity of these reputed Babylonian traditions were questioned, and the doubts connected with them seriously detracted from their value for purposes of criticism. Investigation received new impetus and encouragement from that notable series of brilliant discoveries which were begun, it may be said without invidious comparison, by George Smith. Documents of great age, written in cuneiform characters, were unearthed which both confirmed the general trustworthiness of the Greek citations which have been mentioned, and demonstrated that much, perhaps all, of the doctrine taught in Israel concerning primitive times was an inheritance from Babylonia.

These native records have illuminated and elucidated the early chapters of Genesis. They have established the antiquity of the Hebrew narratives as traditions, with all that this fact involves for interpretation, and they have contributed particulars of greater or less value, which were wanting in the Hebrew record, but which serve to at least cast a side light and sometimes to make methods and conceptions plain which before were obscure or ambiguous.

But along with the valuable material which has been obtained from these records of the past, much that is worthless has been dragged into publicity. Mistranslations, due in part to the infancy of the science of Assyriology and in part to undue haste, have been put forward, meaning has been wrested from the narratives which they were never intended to bear, and false conclusions have been drawn; and these errors have gained currency in popular literature and have been made the basis of argument in works which assume to speak with authority on biblical matters.

The purpose of this book is to attempt the removal of the accumulated rubbish and expose the true material; and when the work of separation has been accomplished as thoroughly as possible, to subject the genuine materials to careful investigation. In not a few instances the Hebrew narrative still stands alone, no parallel account having been found in the literature of other nations. When such is the case, the attempt is made to discover the meaning of the record in the manner of ordinary exegesis, with all the aid afforded by early Hebrew understanding of the tradition. It is regretted that on several topics negative results only can be obtained; but patience with negative results and the quiet tarrying by the argument for and against are better than haste.

The so-called Non-Semitic Version of the Creation-Story has not been introduced into the discussion. The text of this document has not been published, so far as the writer knows, but it has been rendered into English by so competent a translator as Mr. Pinches, of the British Museum. It has not been compared in these pages with the Hebrew records, because it is not a formal and orderly account of creation, but merely constitutes the introduction to a dedicatory prayer uttered on occasion, apparently, of the building or repairing of the great temple of Esagila in Babylon and its numerous sanctuaries. Being the introductory remarks to the prayer, it fittingly recalls moments of creation, beginning in the time before the earth was, by which a place was prepared for that famous seat of worship. It contains references to creation, just as do the eighth Psalm and the thirty-eighth chapter of Job and the second chapter of Genesis. In fact, it forms a strict parallel to these passages, notably to the latter one as this has been traditionally interpreted, in that it gives a *résumé* of such events in the history of creation as were appropriate to introduce the subject in hand.

It remains to be said that the chapter on the creation of the universe is reprinted in the present volume almost verbatim from the pages of the Presbyterian and Reformed Review for July, 1892. The chapter on the flood appeared originally in the tenth volume of the Presbyterian Review, but it has been revised and considerably enlarged for the present publication.

J. D. D.

AUGUST 17, 1894.

CONTENTS

LIST OF ILLUSTRATIONS

GENESIS AND SEMITIC TRADITION

I

THE CREATION OF THE UNIVERSE

FROM the broken and scattered remains of ancient Assyrian and Babylonian literature there has been recovered, as is well known, a story of creation, notable for its striking resemblance to the Hebrew account. The narrative exists in mutilated condition, it is true ; nevertheless, since it was written on a series of tablets, each of which contained the title of the complete work, the number to indicate its place in the series, and a catch-line with the opening words of the succeeding plate, the rearrangement of the fragments in their original order is possible, and with that is established the succession of incidents in the story as once told.[1]

The account begins with a primitive chaos.

"At the time when on high the heaven announced not,
Below the earth named not a name,
  [That is to say : When heaven and earth did not exist]
Then primeval ocean, their generator, [and]
Mummu Tiâmat [the watery deep], the bearer of their totality,
United their waters as one."

. . . .

[1] Translations of the text, inclusive of Rassam's additions, are offered, though of course with many reservations, in English by Sayce, Records of the Past, new series, vol. i., 122 seq., and in German by Jensen, Kosmologie der Babylonier, S. 268 ff.

The origin of the gods was next narrated, but unfortunately the tablet is broken off obliquely at this point, and the ends of several lines carried away. The remnants state that

"At the time when none of the gods had been brought into existence,
[When] a name had not been named, destiny not determined,
Then were made the gods   .   .   .   .   :   .   .   .
The gods Lachmu and Lachamu were brought into existence   .
And grew up .   .   .   .
Anshar and Kishar were made .   .   .   .
Many days passed by .   .   .   .
God Anu [was then made]   .   .   .   ."

This portion of the story has been told in Greek by the neo-platonist Damascius, who had opportunities for learning it, if not in the schools of Alexandria and Athens, at least during his sojourn at the Persian court. His version goes beyond the tablets in expressly stating the material origin of the gods. With omission of his interpretation, his report is that

"The Babylonians assumed two principles of the universe, Tauthe and Apason [i.e., Tiamat and Apsu]; making Apason the husband of Tauthe and naming her the mother of the gods. Of these two there was born an only-begotten son, Moymis. From these same another generation proceeded, Lache and Lachos. Then also from the same [original pair] a third generation, Kissare and Assoros; from whom sprang Anos, Illinos, and Aos; and of Aos and Danke Belos was born, the fabricator of the world."

The cuneiform narrative suffers a long interruption at this point, due to breakage and loss of the tablets. When the story is recovered, it appears that trouble has arisen:

Tiamat has done evil to the gods and is now their enemy. Lachamu has become her ally (iii., 31 obv.) and a troop of hideous creatures, eleven in number, stand ready to assist her (iv., 106,

115). Anshar has in vain sent god Anu [heaven] to punish the offenders; Ea [the waters of the earth] has turned back from the mission aghast; and finally Marduk [the rising sun] has been chosen as avenger and hailed as king.

The gods seat their chosen champion in the princely chamber, and assign him dominion over the universe (iv., 14), declare his weapons irresistible (l., 16), proclaim his word all-powerful, furnish him proof thereof (20–26), and bid him go forth and slay Tiamat (31).

Marduk thereupon arms himself; grasps a spear in his right hand, hangs bow and quiver on his side (37–38), places lightning in front of him, fills his body with flames; he prepares a net to cast over the foe, takes in hand the four winds, arouses a hurricane, an evil wind, a storm, a tempest, the four winds, the seven winds, the cyclone. He sends forth the seven winds in advance to confuse Tiamat, while he himself takes the storm, his great weapon, mounts his war chariot (50), and in the sight of the gods sets out to meet the monster (60). He finds her and challenges her to battle (86). She at once arms, and the combatants approach. Marduk spreads his net around her; releases a hurricane against her which enters her open mouth and prevents her lips from closing, fills her body with a strong wind, pierces her with his spear, grasps and slays her, casts her body down and stands upon it. Leaving the slain Tiamat, he turns his attention to her hideous troop, at once routs them, pursues, captures, and binds them and destroys their weapons.

Having established Anshar's superiority over the enemy, he returned to the body of Tiamat, cleft it in twain and with one half overshadowed the heavens (made a covering for the heavens), then shoved in a bolt, and also set a watchman with orders not to allow the waters to stream forth. Having placed the heavens opposite the watery abyss, he measured the latter and founded an edifice like unto Ishara, like the palace Ishara, which he had built as heaven; and let Anu, Bel, and Ea occupy their dwellings. Then he embellished the heavens, prepared places for the great gods, made the stars, set the zodiac, founded a place for Nibiru, fixed the poles and opened gates provided with locks on either side.

He caused the moon to shine forth and subjected the night to it, he laid the duty upon it every month without fail to mark off [time] with its crown, at the beginning of the month to show horns at evening, on the seventh day to reveal half the crown, on the fourteenth day to stand opposite.

The remainder of this tablet is too broken to admit of connected translation.

One more small fragment of the series exists, but its place in the set is not known further than that, judged by its contents, it must follow those already mentioned. It narrates only the creation of plants (possibly) and animals. Any reference to man it may have contained is broken off. According to it,

"When the gods in their assembly created, they (?) made strong tree trunks (?) brought forth living [crea]tures . . . cattle of the field, [beasts] of the field, and creeping things. . . ."

Such is the story of creation as told by the tablets. But, as is well known, the teaching of the Babylonians was also committed to writing by Berosus, priest of Bel. A portion of the priest's account was cited by Alexander Polyhistor and quoted from his writings by Eusebius and Georgius Syncellus. In these citations the Babylonian priest states that, according to the doctrine of his fellow-countrymen,

"There was a time when nothing existed but darkness and water, wherein resided most hideous beings which were produced of a twofold principle. For men were begotten with two wings; some, moreover, with four wings and two faces and having one body, but two heads, the one that of a man, the other that of a woman, and being in their several organs both male and female; and yet other men appeared, some with the limbs and horns of goats, others with the feet of horses, others with the hind-quarters of a horse and the body of a man, resembling in shape the hippocentaurs. Bulls likewise were bred there with the heads of men, and dogs with four bodies terminated in their extremities with the tails of fishes, and horses with the heads of dogs, and men and other animals with the heads and bodies of horses and the tails of fishes. In short, there were creatures which combined the shapes of all sorts of animals; and in addition to these were fishes, rep-

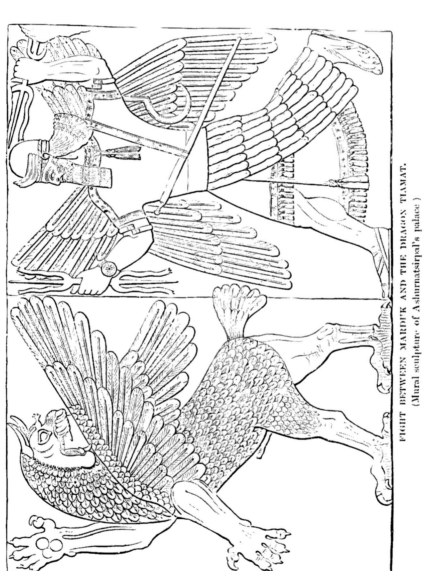

FIGHT BETWEEN MARDUK AND THE DRAGON TIAMAT.
(Mural sculpture of Ashurnatsirpal's palace.)

tiles, serpents, and other animals monstrous and transformed in that they had each other's faces. Representations of these are preserved in the temple of Bel.

"A woman presided over all these by name Omoroka, which in the Chaldean language is θαλατθ,[1] but in Greek is interpreted the sea (θάλασσα), or, as it might be equally well rendered, the moon. When all things were in this condition, Bel came, cut the woman asunder, of one half of her formed the earth and of the other half the heavens, and destroyed the animals which were within her. All this, he says, was an allegorical description of nature; for the whole universe consisting of moisture and animals having been generated therein, the deity above mentioned removed his own head, and the other gods mixed the outflowing blood with earth and formed men; wherefore they are intelligent and partake of divine thought. Now this Bel, by whom they signify Zeus, cleft [as has already been stated in more allegorical language] the darkness asunder, separated earth and heaven from each other, and reduced the universe to order. Now the [nondescript] animals, since they were not able to endure the power of the light, perished. Bel thereupon, seeing a waste but fertile region, commanded one of the gods to remove his [Bel's] head and mix the earth with the thence-flowing blood, and form men and beasts capable of enduring the air. Bel, moreover, made stars and sun and moon and the five planets."

No argument is needed to prove that Berosus and Damascius and the scribe who wrote the tablets have the same story in mind. The fact is patent that these tales are outcroppings of one and the same tradition; a tradition, furthermore, which extends through many ages, and whose traces may be followed back into remote antiquity. The neo-platonist philosopher wrote his concise version about the year 560 after Christ. The priest Berosus penned his account nine hundred years earlier, in the days of Alexander the Great; but even then tablets containing the cuneiform account were old. They had been lying buried for three centuries beneath the ruins of

---

[1] In uncials ΘΛΛΛΤΘ, which Robertson Smith happily conjectures to be a misreading of ΘΛΜΤΕ, tâmtu (ZA. 1891, S. 339).

Nineveh, having been prepared for Ashurbanipal about 650 years before Christ (colophon of fifth tablet). But the story in some form was current earlier still. The conflict of Marduk and the dragon was depicted on the sculptured mural slabs of the palace which Ashurnatsirpal built at Calah 880 years before Christ. Yet more ancient was the restoration of Marduk's temple at Babylon, which Agukakrime undertook. This king reigned later than 1050 B.C. (Delitzsch, 1883), or more probably before the beginning of the fifteenth century B.C. (Tiele, 1885 ; Bezold, 1886 ; Sayce, 1888 ; Guide to British Museum, 1890). The royal restorer relates that he decorated the temple doors with certain objects which he names, and which prove to be the hideous beings allied with Tiamat. Besides these more important monuments of which the date is known, there are numerous undated cylinder seals, covering fairly well the entire period of Assyro-Babylonian civilization, engraven with various scenes from the story and revealing thereby the wide publicity and popularity of the tale. Jensen surmises an earlier date than the earliest which has been mentioned. He argues that the progress of the returning sun of spring among the constellations, placed and named as they are, and its position at the autumnal equinox repeat the story of the conflict of Marduk with Tiamat and her allies ; and hence that the starry host received these names when they occupied such a position with reference to the sun that with his appearance at the vernal equinox the story began. This event, he finds, was not later than 3000 B.C., and concludes that the creation legends are, in part at least, as old as that (Kosmologie, S. 309 320).

A tradition which was current among the inhabitants of the Tigris and lower Euphrates valleys for several thousand years would be known and might perhaps be entertained by people who had been brought under the influence of Babylonian culture. Our main interest in the Babylonian tale centres in its possible affiliation with other cosmogonies, especially with the Hebrew account of creation. Greater or less differences develop themselves in a tradition in the ordinary course of transmission, a fact which is abundantly exemplified by the variations of the Babylonian legend in Babylonia itself. It is not surprising, therefore, that even on the assumption of common origin, in the Assyro-Babylonian and Hebrew traditions of creation, after their subjection to diverse conditions, differences obtrude themselves. There is literary unlikeness. The Babylonian story knows nothing of a division into days (see Presbyterian Review, vol. x., 670 seq.) ; whereas the Hebrew account is distributed within a framework of six days. The Babylonian tale, moreover, not only encumbers the plain narrative of creation with an account of the choice and exaltation of a demiurge and of his preparation for the mission, but it is, to say the least, highly figurative and to the last degree anthropomorphic ; the Hebrew story, on the other hand, is the sober recital in simple, yet stately prose of the impressive tradition concerning the development of the ordered universe from chaos. In addition to the marked literary contrasts there is a profound difference in conception. The Babylonian stories taken together describe the primeval waters as spontaneously generative ; the Hebrew account represents the material of the universe as lying waste and lifeless, and as not assuming order or becoming productive of life until the going forth of the divine command. These divergent views are allied with the different theistic conceptions of the two peoples. On this subject the fragments of Berosus' narrative throw no light. He is describing the origin of the ordered universe and assumes the existence of the gods, however he may have treated of them in his complete history, mentioning them only casually in connection with their respective activities in the work of creation. The cuneiform story goes back to a time when the gods did not exist. It depicts the primeval chaos of waters and proceeds to state, without determining the manner of origination, that the gods came into being in successive periods of long duration and in the order assigned by Damascius. The tradition as reported by the latter ascribes a material origin to the gods; the primeval waters producing among others an early pair of deities, from which the other gods were descended by successive generations—a conception which is, perhaps, allied to the Phœnician doctrine that out of the material of the universe were evolved sun, moon, stars and constellations which eventually arrived at consciousness and were called the watchers of heaven. In the Hebrew records, however, a different theistic doctrine prevails. God is the creator of the heavens and the earth, the bringer into existence of that which did not previously exist. Before the mountains were brought forth, or ever he had formed the earth and the world, even from everlasting to everlasting he is God. He was from the beginning or ever the earth was, when there were no depths, no t'hômôth, no ti'âmâti (Prov. viii. 22–24).

But this difference in conceptions, diametrically opposed though these views be, is explicable without denial of kinship between the accounts so soon as the divergent thought of the two peoples is recalled. And two considerations leave no reasonable doubt of a relationship between the two traditions: first, the ancient common habitat in Babylonia of the two peoples who transmitted these accounts; and second, the community of conception, Hebrews and Babylonians uniting in describing the prim-

itive condition of the universe as an abyss of waters
shrouded in darkness and subsequently parted in twain
in order to the formation of heaven and earth. The kinship between the traditions need not be close, but kinship there is.

The question then is, How are these two traditions related to the original source? An answer is offered by
the mediation theory, which regards the Babylonian legend as intermediate in time and as forming the connecting link between the primitive story and its assumed Hebrew modification. According to this theory, the early
tradition, ever changing, passed through the elaborate
Babylonian tale and thence into the purified Hebrew
form. The prevalent opinion is expressed by Jensen,
who declares that "the end of the fourth and the fragments of the fifth and seventh (?) tablets, together with
the beginning of the first, quite unquestionably form the
prototype of the biblical legends" (Kosmologie, S. 304).
Notice that, in addition to the opening lines in the
first tablet which depict the primitive condition of the
universe as watery chaos, the part of the Babylonian tale
which is declared to form the prototype of the biblical
story is that portion which is taken up with the description of the work of Marduk as fabricator of the universe
(S. 304-306). The monotheistic revisers, finding nothing
objectionable in the conception, allowed the description
of the universe to remain, which represented it as once
existing in a state of chaotic waters enshrouded in darkness. The story of the origin of the gods, believers in
one god necessarily omitted, and took up the tale again
with the work of the demiurge, Marduk, the *light bringer*,
whom they simply identified with the one eternal God.
Following the order of the Babylonian narrative, they next
related the separation of the waters and formation of
heaven ; then the gathering of the lower waters into one

place and the appearance of the dry land ; then, departing for a moment from the Babylonian order, the clothing of earth's surface with vegetation ; then, once more like the Babylonian narrative, the creation of the heavenly bodies and the calling forth of animate terrestrial beings. The Babylonian tale was thus, it is claimed, stripped of all features repugnant to the spirit of monotheism, reduced to a fundamental though modified physical conception, and transfused and glorified with the doctrine of the eternal God, creator and sovereign of the universe.

This mediation theory, however, rests, we believe, on a demonstrable error. Contrary to the common assumption, the Hebrew narrative is not chiefly, if it is at all, reflected in the Marduk section of the cuneiform story, but in the first tablet and in Damascius. It shines conspicuously in the lineage which is assigned to the gods by these authorities, for the genealogical succession of the gods is the creational order of the natural objects which they were supposed to animate. Damascius, it will be remembered, reports the Babylonian belief that at first there were two principles of the universe, viz., the two primeval waters ; from which, as from parents, sprang not only Moymis and the gods Lachmu and Lachamu, but also two others, related as children of the same generation, Kishar and Anshar, which being interpreted mean the comprehensive heavens above and the comprehensive earth beneath ; and of these in turn came a group of three—Anu, heaven, and Illinos, earth's surface, and Ea, the terrestrial waters ; and the son of the latter, so called because rising daily from that god's abode, the ocean, was Bel [Marduk], the sun, whom the Babylonians say is the demiurge. Evidently if for these divinities there be substituted the natural objects which the divine names signify, an orderly statement is rendered, like that in the book of Genesis, of the physical development of the universe. A similar doctrine permeates the native literature. According to the monuments Gur, *i.e.* Apsu, the primeval ocean, was "the mother, the bearer of heaven and earth" (II R., 54, 18c; ASKT., 76, 15/16), "the mother of Anu and the gods" (Ancient History from the Monuments: Babylonia, p. 66, note; RP., vol. ix., 146, 64, note). Of these Anu, Bel, *i.e.* Illil or Ἰλλινος, and Ea constituted a triad, the supreme one in the Assyrian pantheon. And of Ea and his consort Damkina, *i.e.* Dauke (II R., 55, 53d), "the king and queen of the watery deep" (II R., 55, 24c.d.), was born Marduk (II R., 55, 64d).

The account as transmitted by the first tablet does not expressly publish the descent of the gods from the primeval waters, as does Damascius, though traces of a traditional genealogy are contained in the later tablets of the series in allusions to the gods as the fathers or ancestors of Marduk. It does, however, purport to give the chronological order in which the gods came into existence. It pictures a primitive chaos of waters, and then proceeds to relate the origin of the deities; teaches, like Damascius, that Lachmu and Lachamu, whoever they may have been and who later became involved with Tiamat, came into existence and grew up; that Anshar and Kishar—in other words that heaven and earth in the widest meaning of these terms, namely, all above and all below—were formed; that after a long period Anu, the spirit of the heavens proper, and Bel, the surface of the earth, and Ea, the terrestrial waters, were made.[1] Here again the substitution for the gods of the natural objects which their names signify and which they were believed to animate yields a correct chronological account of the physical development of the universe. In the light of this evidence, the story which the tablets, espe-

[1] Last two names restored from context and Damascius.

cially in their opening sentences, tell, and which they reveal later between the lines, is not in its germ a sun
myth—although it has unfolded into or been engrafted
on a sun myth (cp. Sayce, Hibbert Lectures, 1887, p.
393)—but it is the deformed outgrowth of an earlier physical doctrine of the origin of the universe.

It may be read later between the lines of the Marduk
section, we say ; for it is legible in Marduk's inferior rank
and in the actual place assigned to him in the pantheon.
The Babylonian religion was a nature worship according
to which natural objects were regarded as animated.
Yet Marduk, the rising sun, who in earliest times was
represented as destroyer of Tiamat, framer of heaven
and earth and seas, and constructor of the abodes of the
gods, was not originally worshipped as father of the gods,
the first in order of time, the head of the pantheon, but
as a subordinate deity ; and when at a late period he
was admitted into the number of the great gods, it was
as occupant of a humble position.   To this fact the story
of creation as told by the tablets—and in a part which
is traceable to the earliest times—bears witness.   The
king of the gods is Anshar; he sends Anu to subdue
Tiamat, and on Anu's failure employs Ea ; and not until
the god of terrestrial waters proves unable does Anshar
turn to Marduk as a last resort.   It is only after this
commission has been announced that Marduk is led into
the princely chamber by the gods, who are called his ancestors, and there endued with might and invested with
dominion over the universe (iv. 14).   This peculiarity
is not accidental, but significant.   The explanation is
found in the underlying cosmological theory : Marduk's
birth immediately followed that of the triad of deities,
Anu (heaven), Bel (earth), and Ea (house of terrestrial
water).   The universe had in part developed before
Marduk came into being ; his rank coincides with his

place in unfolding cosmos, and the order in which the gods one after another are sent forth to battle, the reliance which is placed in Marduk's predecessors before he is appealed to for help, likewise correspond broadly to the chronological succession of the gods as determined by the creative order of the natural objects which they represent. Thus even the Marduk section of the creation story, notwithstanding its representation of that god as a maker of heaven and earth, seems in reality to presuppose a somewhat advanced stage in the formation of the universe before his offices are called into requisition.

With this elucidation in mind, the cuneiform story as a whole should be reviewed. The tale begins with the statement that at first the primeval waters lay mingled together, and eventually became the begetter and bearer of heaven and earth. Deities came into existence : first Lachmu and Lachamu ; then, after a considerable period, all above and all below ; after lapse of other years, heaven, earth's surface, and terrestrial waters ; finally, Marduk, the rising sun.[1] But Tiamat, the watery abyss, resisted the unfolding order and infringed the divine command, probably by her continual endeavor to confound earth and heaven and sea. The nightly darkness obscuring the regions of the universe and enveloping all nature in the primeval shroud, the dense mists reuniting at times the waters of heaven and earth, continued rains when the windows of heaven were opened and the fountains of the great deep broken up, which threatened to deluge the earth and again convert the celestial and terrestrial waters into the one vast original ocean, suggested a possible return to chaos ; yea, *told* these Babylonians who believed in the existence of animate beings back of

[1] Compare the Phœnician tradition that the heavenly bodies were spontaneously developed from the chaotic mass of matter and in process of time arrived at consciousness.

every natural object, of a determined struggle on the
part of Tiamat to reduce all things to primitive disorder;
while the black clouds and vapors of fantastic shape, the
angry mutterings of thunder and the fierce tornado
evoked in their superstitious minds the conception of a
brood of horrid creatures, offspring and abettors of Tiamat, allied with their cruel progenitress in bitter warfare against the established order of the universe. These
foes, which the Babylonians discerned in darkness and
fog and storm, the deity of the comprehensive heavens,
Anshar, attempted in vain to overcome. Ea, lord of
earthly waters, availed still less. Finally Marduk, the
rising sun, was sent. A fearful storm was the result
(Tablet iv., 45 seq.), but the god of the rising sun dis-
pelled the darkness, scattered the hideously shaped
clouds, lifted the vapors in masses on high, subdued the
tempest, reopened the space between heaven and earth,
revealed the blue firmament, cleared a pathway for the
starry host, brought to light the earth and dried its surface, awoke animal and vegetable life.

The story in its developed form is an exaltation of the
sun. The events which preceded the sun's appearance
are recognized; but being apart from the plan are not
dwelt upon. Moreover, in course of time, with the
growth of the mythological conception and the conse-
quent partial concealment of the germ of the tale, there
ultimately developed a story which ascribed to the hero
Marduk results which, even in Babylonian thought, were
in nowise due to the sun's agency (cp. Jensen, Kosmologie, S. 309).

Compare with this Babylonian story the account which
the Israelites transmitted. A striking feature of the
Hebrew narrative is its symmetry. While by necessity
a natural sequence of events is observed, the principle of
grouping prevails. Creative acts, so distinct as to be in-

troduced by the recurring formula, "God said, Let there
be," and dismissed by the statement, "God saw that it
was good;" creative acts so diverse as is making from
creating, or as is the gift of life from the mere separation of the material elements, are in several instances
grouped in one and the same period, as in the first, third,
fifth, and sixth days. Again, the motionless objects are
grouped as the works of the first three days, and the
moving objects—or those which appear to move—the
works of the last three days. Still again, the respective
periods of these two great divisions offset each other :
the creation of light on the first day corresponds to the
making of the heavenly luminaries on the first day of
the second division ; the parting of waters by a firmament
on the second day, to the calling forth of animate beings
in the waters and in front of the firmament on the same
day of the second division ; the appearance of dry land
and of vegetation on the third day, to the land animals
and the appointment of herbs for their food on the third
day of the second division. This distribution of the various works of creation is not arbitrary, but logically
determined ; it is based on the relations of these objects
the one to the other, and it exhibits the true character
and progress and purpose of creation.

Of course the conclusion would be unwarranted that
this symmetry is necessarily artificial; but the theory
that it is the result of intentional arrangement is plausible and has been adopted and advocated by leading in-
terpreters. If entertained, its bearing upon another
question must not be overlooked. If it be true that the
material has been arranged, it follows that while the
natural sequence of events has in a measure been retained in the narrative, chronology has been subordinated ; it has been either intentionally ignored or at
least only so far regarded as that the works of creation,

which may have had their beginning in a prior period, have been recounted in the order of their "day" or period of prominence, not in the order of their coming into existence.

What, then, is meant by the much-discussed days of the Hebrew tradition; for so far as yet appears they are peculiar to the Hebrew transmission?[1] Under the teaching of God, they are the accurate and admirable classification of the works of creation under six divisions; six distinct groups of deeds followed by cessation from creative activity, for the end and ideal of creation had been attained. And in view of the sacredness which was conventionally attached to the number seven, even by the authorized teachers of Israel, seven sections were peculiarly appropriate in a narrative of God's works. And these sections are called days. It is to be admitted that these expressions can, on purely linguistic grounds, be interpreted as ordinary days, which, taken together, form a week of seven times twenty-four hours. It is also to be admitted that, on literary grounds, these terms can be interpreted as days, marked by the alternation of light and darkness, but not consecutive. The several days are the respective points of time when God issued his decrees. No stringent reason compels belief that this same writer would teach that there were ten generations and no more from Adam to Noah and from Shem to Abraham; and certainly Matthew neither believed nor would teach that the generations from Abraham to David and from David to the captivity and from the captivity to Christ were in every case consecutive and in each group were fourteen and no more. Perhaps the Hebrew writer is pursuing the same plan when he describes the six groups of creative deeds as the works of six several days, and adds thereto the seventh day of

[1] The Etruscan story is of course not forgotten.

divine rest; thus making, when taken together, a complete week and a heavenly example to men of labor and repose. Still again it is to be admitted with Driver, Delitzsch, and a host of other distinguished scholars, that "the writer may have consciously used the term [day] figuratively," for the words day and week were unquestionably employed by the Hebrews with latitude. It has, indeed, been argued that the periphrastic division of the day into two halves bounded by evening and morning is conclusive proof that an ordinary day of twenty-four hours is meant (Dillmann); but if day is used figuratively, evening and morning must likewise be, and accordingly the answer has been well returned that evening may mean " the time when the Creator brought his work [temporarily] to a close, and morning the time when the creative activity began anew " (Delitzsch). Each period of creative activity was followed by one of inactivity, corresponding to night when man works not; and when creation was complete, when the ideal which God had set before him had been attained, when all had been pronounced very good, God entered upon his long and as yet unended Sabbath of cessation from creative work, or, as the writer himself significantly phrases it, from " work which God made in a creative manner."

Three interpretations of the term day are accordingly in themselves admissible, and we are constrained to join others in saying with Augustine : " What kind of days these were it is extremely difficult or perhaps impossible for us to conceive and how much more to say ! " (De civ. Dei, xi., 6). A breadth of statement is employed by the author which is usual with biblical writers when setting forth the subordinate elements of their doctrine and which renders the teaching of Scripture broader than the varying conceptions which man in different ages entertains.

2

The writer's own conception, not of day, but of the time occupied in bringing the world into its present condition, may be ascertained, if not with certainty, at least with probability. The plausibility of the theory that he subordinates time to arrangement has already been mentioned. Add to that the fitting omission of the definite article from the enumeration of the periods: day one, day second, day third, day fourth, day fifth, and, to judge from the versions, day sixth; leaving the expressions in themselves indefinite, which is not customary when, as here, ordinals are used and the days of an ordinary week-period are numbered (Num. xxix. 17, 20, 23, etc.; Neh. viii. [2], 13, 18; cp. Num. vii. 12, etc., et pass.). The method of enumeration employed is suitable for exhibiting a relation between the groups which the writer would not narrowly define; and accordingly he speaks of a second day, a third day, etc. Add further the Semitic tradition which has been preserved in the Babylonian version that the successive stages in the development of the ordered universe occupied long periods of untold duration, and the presumption becomes strong that the Hebrew writer likewise conceived of the creation period, not as seven times twenty-four hours, but as vastly, indefinitely long.

So much for the style and for the framework of the Hebrew tradition. Now as to its contents. The cosmology underlying the Hebrew account, apart from its theology, is that at first there was a chaos: called the earth, because the heavens had not yet been detached from the mass, and because it contained all the elements out of which the universe was formed; called also the great deep, or *t'hôm*, because existing in watery or fluid state. This mass of material was shrouded in darkness. Then light was created. All accounts, Babylonian and Hebrew, presuppose the existence of light before the sun.

The idea was familiar to the ancients, being found among the Aryans east and west as well as among the Semites. The doctrine is true; the causes were of old at work which make the light of myriad suns and render our own orb of day luminous. Then the blue vault called the firmament parted the primeval waters, dividing the fluid heavens from the fluid earth. The latter watery body is next described as undergoing change; it was separated into seas and dry land, and the land clothed with verdure. As yet, however, notwithstanding the allusion to vegetation, no mention has been made of the creation of the sun. In this the Hebrew departs from the Babylonian order of narration, which tells of the formation of the sun and stars immediately after that of earth and before any allusion has been made to vegetation. The explanation may be found either in the author's intention to teach that vegetation preceded the sun's formation or at least the sun's appearance through the mists, or else in his method of grouping already described. It may be that the author, without intending to teach the priority of vegetation to the sun's light and heat, having narrated the gathering together of the terrestrial waters and the appearance of dry land, wished to preserve the determined symmetry of his account and to complete the present picture by telling of the verdure which forthwith covered the earth, and which in reality forms one stage with the ground in the earth's development. It may be added in passing that perhaps no man to this day knows whether vegetation delayed until the sun had thrown off the planets which are within the earth's orbit and had assumed its present dimensions, or whether herbage appeared long before. Proceeding now to the movable bodies, the Hebrew narrator first describes those which pass in solemn procession across the sky—the sun, moon, and stars. Then he depicts as a succeeding day the time when fish swarmed in the waters, and fowl flew in the heaven, when the lower animals reached great development and dominated the earth. He pictures next the day of the land animals, made of the earth, higher in order of being than fish or fowl, attaining to prominence and dominion after the reign of aquatic and aërial animals, and culminating in man, created in the same manner as were they, ruling at the same time with them on earth, but made in the divine image and commissioned to subdue the earth to himself and reign supreme among its creatures.

The outcroppings of the Semitic tradition of the creation of the world, as they come to light on the Tigris and the lower Euphrates and in Palestine, reveal a diverging trend in southern Mesopotamia. The original tradition, discoverable even beneath the distortions to which it was subjected by polytheism, represented a primitive condition of the universe consisting of chaotic waters enveloped in darkness; a separation of these so-called waters into two divisions, the great above and the great beneath; the clear distinction, later, of these into heaven above and land and ocean beneath. Under the influence of animistic nature worship, however, this fundamental physical doctrine was perverted. The divisions of the universe were severally assigned a spirit and deified; consequently the original teaching of the orderly development of the material universe became in allegory the genealogy of the gods. At the point where the appearance of the sun was noted, the tradition diverged still more. The worshippers of the one true God, preserving both the physical doctrine and the sublime truth behind it, told of the appearance, at God's command, of sun, moon, and stars, of animate beings in sea and air, of beasts on earth and of man in the divine image. The Assyro-Babylonian adorers of nature, on the other hand, worshipping the sun, hail him as offspring of ocean's lord and lady, because going forth daily from the sea, laud him as the restorer and preserver of order and the awakener of life; yea, they exalt him at length to the rank of creator, and in their fervor ascribe to him the completion of the universe. The physical doctrine, which is the substratum of the tradition, has been preserved in the Hebrew transmission. The deification of nature and the glorification of the sun are polytheistic amplifications. The Hebrew account is the intentional perpetuation of the basal doctrine of the origin of the universe.

And now allow the eye to sweep in rapid survey over the literature of antiquity. Cosmological theories entertained by the peoples who were akin or neighbor or by commerce and conquest bound to the Babylonians, Assyrians, and Hebrews come to light. In Etruria and Greece, in Persia, India, Egypt, and Phœnicia cosmogonies are found which bear resemblances to the Semitic tradition; concurring with it not in the accidents of literary form and mythological fancies, but in the essential of physical doctrine. For the most part they, too, like the Babylonian tale, find a place for the sun and exaggerate his agency; and yet not one is a sun myth. The exact relationship of these cosmogonies to the Semitic tradition cannot as yet be finally determined; but all confirmation which, with increasing knowledge of ancient thought, shall accrue that these teachings have a common origin with the Babylonian and Hebrew transmission is additional proof that the genealogy of the gods is a distortion and the sun myth an amplification of the primitive tradition.

These national traditions show more. They show that the original doctrine was never wholly lost sight of by mankind at large. It was an influential presence in human thought. But especially among the ancient Baby-

lonians was the primitive tradition apprehended despite
its perversion; for the same agencies which distorted
worked also to preserve it. The early doctrine of the
more or less vital relation between the gods and the
natural objects whose names they bore and which they
inhabited, a doctrine which had converted the account of
the physical development of the universe into the genealogical descent of the gods, must act in the opposite direction; the genealogy of the gods must be ever readily
reconvertible into the generations of the heavens and the
earth. Whenever, then, this primitive, ever-discernible,
and imperishable teaching of the origin of the universe
was held by monotheists, it was formulated essentially
as is the doctrine in the opening chapter of the book of
Genesis.

II

THE SABBATH

EIGHTEEN years ago Mr. Fox Talbot, one of the first successful translators of the Assyrian inscriptions, announced to the public his opinion that in the fifth tablet of the creation series the Babylonians clearly affirmed "the origin of the Sabbath" to have been "coeval with creation." He found on that tablet these remarkable lines :

"Every month without fail he [*i.e.* God] made holy assembly-days.

. . . .

On the seventh day he appointed a holy day
And to cease from all business he commanded."
(RP., vol. ix., 117, 118; cp. TSBA., vol. v., 428.)

Increased knowledge of the Assyrian vocabulary has, however, made it certain that the version given by the eminent translator is inaccurate at crucial points. The word *ayû*, which he boldly guessed to mean holy assembly-day (thinking of the Hebrew *chag*), is now known to signify a crown or, as Jensen prefers to describe it, a royal cap ; and the passage proves to be a description, not of the institution of the Sabbath, but of the moon's changes. A translation which is nearer to the sense of the original is :

"He caused the moon to shine forth, he subjected the night to it,
He made it known as an object of the night. In order to make known the days
Every month without fail mark off [time (?)] with the crown ;

At the beginning of the month, on rising at evening,
Horns thou dost show in order to make known the heaven,
On the seventh day the crown . . . ."

About the time that this text came to light, a discovery was made which has awakened wide interest. The phrase "day of rest of heart," as the words have been translated, was found in an Assyrian vocabulary and by its side its synonym was given as *Shabattu*. This fact naturally attracted attention. But it was early abused. Without any warrant save that of plausibility to justify the procedure, it was combined with a peculiar feature of a ritualistic calendar, which is presently to be mentioned, and the announcement was published—not as a conjecture, but as a fact—that the word Sabbath was known to the Assyrians, was the name given to the seventh, fourteenth, nineteenth, twenty-first, and twenty-eighth day of each month, and was "explained as 'a day of rest for the heart'" (Sayce, *Academy*, Nov., 1875, p. 554, *Babylonian Literature*, p. 55; Schrader, KAT²., S. 18 ff.; Tiele, *Babylonisch-assyrische Geschichte*, S. 550). But these statements are bold assumptions. The pronunciation of the word as *Shabattu* is not quite certain. The signs which compose it may be so read; but they may likewise be pronounced *Shabêtu* or *Shamittu* or *Shapattu*. One reading is as likely as another. There is no inherent reason for a preference. *Shabattu* has been adopted solely because it is a suitable synonym of the phrase "day of rest of heart." But here, again, a question must be raised. The phrase *nuch libbi*, which has been translated "rest of heart," is of frequent occurrence in Assyrian literature in this form or a variation of it, being employed to signify the appeasing of the heart of the gods. This meaning must be retained in the passage under discussion unless other facts come to light (cp. Jensen, ZA., vol. iv., 274). The utmost that this celebrated line yields is that a day of propitiation was possibly called Sabbath. From aught that appears, it was neither a day of rest nor the recurring seventh day, but any season devoted to appeasing an angry god.

Reference has been made to a ritualistic calendar. The first tablet of the kind was discovered in the year 1869 by that enthusiastic Assyriologist of former days, Mr. George Smith, while at work upon the heap of miscellaneous fragments of clay and stone tablets which had come into possession of the British Museum (Assyrian Discoveries, p. 12). It was a religious calendar for the intercalary month of second Elul, and indicated for each day in succession the deity of the day, the festival to be celebrated, the offerings to be made, and occasionally the proper deportment of men. But these regulations were not peculiar to intercalary Elul. In their main provisions they were common to all the months of the year. Numerous similar tablets have come to light which show that the corresponding days of the various months were distinguished by the same festivals, the same commands, and the same prohibitions.

The feature which lends to these calendars their great interest is the special notice taken of the recurring seventh day. On the seventh, fourteenth, nineteenth, twenty-first, and twenty-eighth day of each month certain acts are forbidden. The prohibitions are the same for each of these days. The law was this:

" The seventh day, a festival of the god Marduk and the goddess Zarpanitu.[1] A propitious day. [Nevertheless] an unlucky day: the shepherd of many nations shall not eat meat[2] which has been cooked on the fire . . ., the raiment of his body he shall not change, nor put on clean clothing, nor make a libation; the king shall not ride in his chariot nor speak as a ruler; the

[1] The deities are different on each of the recurring seventh days.
[2] " Anything," nineteenth day.

priest shall not carry on a conversation in a secret place ; the seer shall not lay his hand on the sick, nor stretch it forth to call down a curse. At night [1] in the presence of god Marduk and goddess Ishtar the king shall make his offering, pour out his libation ; the lifting up of his hands unto god will be acceptable."

How striking is the resemblance to the Jewish Sabbath ! The shepherd of many nations—the proud title in Babylonia and Assyria of the grand monarch who swayed his sceptre over a vast empire of mixed and subjugated peoples—the shepherd of many nations is warned not to eat cooked meat on the recurring seventh day ; and it was a statute in Israel that the people should neither bake, nor seethe, nor kindle a fire throughout their habitations on the Sabbath, and the man who gathered sticks in the wilderness on that day was stoned (Ex. xvi. 23 ; xxxv. 3 ; Num. xv. 32–36). The Assyrian king is warned not to ride in his chariot on the seventh day, and the Jews restricted the distance that might be travelled on that day. The king is warned not to speak as a ruler, which seems to mean that he must neither legislate nor judge ; and according to the rabbis cases at law might not be tried on the Sabbath, save when the offence was against religion. In Assyria the seer must not apply his hand to the sick ; and the scribes and Pharisees found fault with Jesus of Nazareth because he healed the sick on the Sabbath day.

These common points, however, prove nothing. Notwithstanding them, the Hebrew law may possibly have no connection with the precepts of this particular Assyrian ritual. The resemblance is indeed great, but the contrasts are greater. The day set apart was not the same in both countries, the controlling idea of the day was different and the practice was different.

1. There was a difference as to the day. In Assyria

[1] "In the morning," twenty-first day.

significance attached to that day of the month which was seven or its multiple. Among the Israelites it was independent of the day of the month, being the recurring seventh day in unbroken succession throughout the year.[1] In other words, among the Assyrians it was always the seventh, fourteenth, nineteenth, twenty-first and twenty-eighth days of the month which were marked by these regulations, while the Hebrew Sabbath might fall on any day of the month. The difference as to the day is, it is true, of minor importance ; for it is conceivable that it arose by simple substitution, parallel to the historic change of the Sabbath from the seventh to the first day of the week : nevertheless the difference is characteristic and may be profoundly significant.

2. Again, a different conception of the day prevailed in the two countries. Every feature of the Jewish observance, even the minutest, both before the period of Babylonian influence and after the exile, is based on the theory that the Sabbath is a day of rest from labor. There was a deeper thought. The Creator rested on the seventh day and in his benevolence blessed it and hallowed it that all his creatures might enjoy like rest. The Sabbath should be a benediction to man's physical being and woo his soul to greater love for God.

This pure and sublime truth stands in marked contrast to the Assyrian theory. In Assyria the recurring seventh day of the month was not a sacred day, but merely an unlucky day. The prohibitions which are found in the ritual are not laws, but warnings. Man is not forbidden, but cautioned. The deeds prohibited are not wrong, but dangerous. It is unlucky for the king to

---

[1] The law speaks of a period of six days intervening between the Sabbaths. The fifty days which elapsed between the offering of the sheaf of the first fruits and Pentecost included the ends of two months and yet including the next morning numbered seven weeks.

ride in his chariot on that day, unlucky for the priest to converse in private, unlucky for the seer to stretch forth his hand to touch the sick.

What gave to the day this dismal character? Unpropitiousness was no uncommon characteristic of times and seasons in Assyria. The Assyrians regarded days when it was inauspicious to eat fish, dangerous to pay money, unfortunate to ride in a ship, lucky to kill a snake. They noted and catalogued the months as lucky or unlucky for going to camp or engaging in battle (III R., 52). They watched the varying aspects of the moon because they thought that they discerned portents of good or evil in lunar phenomena. The sole peculiarity of the calendar under consideration is that unlucky acts are noted for the recurring seventh and the nineteenth day of the month.

The phasing of the moon has properly been thought of as the possible explanation for the separation of these days from all others. The radiant orb of night has served many peoples as a heavenly clock, measuring off the month and dividing it into seven-day periods. But in the ritualistic calendar the months are not lunar, but contain thirty days; and the unlucky days fall on the same date every month. The ill-fated day might fairly coincide with the phases of the moon in Nisan; but the divergence between the recurring seventh day and the moon's quarter would be quite apparent to the eye in the second month, and the variation would increase as the months rolled on. The nineteenth day of the month, too, was regarded with the same superstitious awe as the recurring seventh day. There is no possible relation between the nineteenth day of the month and the quartering of the moon.

A similar argument opposes the theory that, a week of seven days having been adopted because of the seven great luminaries in the heavens, the baleful character of the seventh day was due to its association with the gloomy planet Saturn. The theory falls short of an explanation ; for it, too, fails to account for the like regard being paid to the nineteenth day of the month as to the recurring seventh.

The evidence at present available indicates that the thought uppermost in man's mind when these ritualistic tablets took final form was the dread with which the number seven was invested. The feeling of awe which was associated with it accounts for the separation not only of the recurring seventh day of the month, but also of the nineteenth day, the seventh seventh from the beginning of the preceding month (Boscawen). By this means they apologized in a measure for the slight put upon the recurring seventh when the twenty-ninth and thirtieth days were left out of the calculation.

3. The day was differently observed by the two peoples. The execution of the offender in the wilderness, the song for the Sabbath day, promises and threats of prophets, city gates closed and traffic stopped, towns preferring capture and armies submitting to massacre rather than engage even in defensive warfare on the Sabbath, tell how Israel kept the appointed day of rest. A far different state of things prevailed on the Tigris. The Assyrians and Babylonians did not keep the unlucky seventh day as a national Sabbath. It was not kept by the people as a day of rest. Armies marched forth to begin a campaign and war was waged on that day (III R., 8, 78 ; Babylonian Chronicle, col. iii., 3). Numerous dated tablets bear unintentional testimony that barter and trade went on as usual ; that the formalities of sale, the assembling of witnesses, and the signing of documents proceeded without interruption ; that the laborious work of engraving inscriptions had no cessation. One copy of

the annals of Ashurbanipal, filling ten long columns, is, in whole or in part, the work of the twenty-eighth day of Elul (III R., 26, 122). There is no truth in the assertions that the calendar described "Sabbaths on which no work was allowed to be done" and that these days "were kept like the Jewish Sabbath" (Smith, Chaldean Account of Genesis, p. 89; Sayce, Ancient Empires, p. 171). Without doubt the calendar must be understood literally; the recurring seventh day was unlucky, not for the people at large, but for the king, the priest and the seer, and for the specified acts only.[1]

The differences in the day set apart, in the theory and in the practice, are so marked as to raise a doubt whether the unlucky day of this Assyrian ritual had any connection whatsoever with the Hebrew Sabbath. Francis Brown questions, yet rather favors, the theory of some historical connection (Presbyterian Review, vol. iii., p. 688 seq.). Jensen denies any *direct* connection (S. S. Times, 1892, p. 35 seq.). Final decision may be postponed. Unquestionably the Assyrian ritual does not represent the Sabbath of Israel; and yet it may have a common origin. It may be the degenerate relic of a better law. The prohibition of secular work may have once been attached to the day, but been gradually ignored, as the fourth commandment has been in parts of Christendom and only a superstitious expectation of fatality as attendant upon certain deeds on that day left to tell of the nobler past. Especially may this be true, if traces of a conception of the seventh day as auspicious or sabbatic can be found in the older Babylonian literature. The theory that in early ages secular work was generally proscribed on the seventh day would at any rate account for both the Assyrian calendar and the Sinaitic legislation.

---

[1] It is noteworthy as a commentary on Babylonian custom that the children of Israel brought back habits of seventh-day labor from the captivity.

Thus far investigation has done little but clear away the fogs in which the question has unfortunately been allowed to become involved. Several facts, important because of their bearing upon the question of the origin and early observance of the Sabbath, may now, it is hoped, be looked at with unobscured vision. One of these is that a seven-day period was a measure of time in vogue among the Semites in remote ages. Not that there is absolute proof of a week in our sense of the term, universally observed, ever sharply defined, one following another in a series in uninterrupted succession throughout the year, a little era by which all people reckon, and within whose bounds they feel themselves living; but only that a period of seven days as a division of time had been thrust on man's notice and kept before his mind by nature or revelation or both, and had found employment in daily life. The Hebrews preserved the tradition that the birds which Noah sent forth from the ark were despatched at intervals of seven days. The Arameans and Philistines had certain marriage observances which lasted seven days (Gen. xxix. 27, 28; Judg. xiv. 12, 17). According to the Babylonian story of the flood, the storm raged six days and six nights and ceased on the seventh day, making a week in all, and the ark lay stranded on the mountain an equal period before man ventured to disembark. Gudea, who was a prince of Lagash long before the days of Moses, celebrated a festival of seven days' duration on the completion of a temple. In the tale of Adapa, son of Ea, a legend which antedates the fifteenth century before Christ, the south wind is said to have ceased to blow for seven days. The week with a conventional beginning which all men reckoned as first day is, of course, not intended in every case. The week which was fulfilled for Leah began on the day of her marriage. The six days and seven nights

of Izdubar's sleep commenced when the stupor over-
powered him. The six days and seven nights of
Eabani's association with his new companion began
when the acquaintance was formed on the second day of
waiting by the drinking-place. But these passages show
that the seven-day period was a recognized standard,
that it was employed for the varied purposes of ordinary life, that it had come to be denoted by the peculiar
formula six days and seven nights (cp. שברע), that it was
used loosely like our week for seven successive days
irrespective of the starting-point; and it is noticeable
that the periods are consecutive in the account of the
flood when Noah sends forth the birds at regular intervals of seven days, and perhaps also in the Babylonian
narrative, where the seven days of storm and fairing
weather are followed by seven days during which the
ship lies aground on the mountain. The duration of
Noah's confinement in the ark, from the day of his entrance to that of his release, is measurable by consecutive weeks, fifty-three in all; and with the exception of
the stranding of the drifting ark, which may be regarded
as an accident of nature, the events that are dated by the
day of the month fall on the first or seventh day of these
consecutive weeks; and it will be shown in connection with the chronology of the flood that perhaps even
the forty days of rain, and again of waiting after the
appearance of the mountain-tops, are bounded by the
first and seventh days of these consecutive seven-day
periods.

What gave rise to this reckoning by a seven-day period? Not improbably the phasing moon had some influence. Men relied upon that occurrence in remotest
antiquity for the measurement of time; for the moon
marked off months and divided them approximately into
seven-day periods with unfailing regularity (Lotz, de

historia Sabbati, p. 37 ; Robertson Smith, Encyc. Brit., Art. Sabbath). The phenomenon is referred to in the passage already quoted from the Creation tablets.

"In order to make known the days
Every month without fail mark off [time (?)] with the crown ;
At the beginning of the month, on rising at night,
Horns dost thou show in order to make known the heaven,
On the seventh day the crown . . . ."

With these lines the words of Genesis may not inaptly be compared as an expression of man's habit of depending on the heavenly bodies in general to measure time for him, and of his apprehension that these bodies were intended by the Creator to serve this purpose. " Let there be lights in the firmament of heaven . . . and let them be for signs and for seasons, and for days and years."

But the moon's changes do not account for the auspicious and sacred character of the seventh day, nor does the additional fact that among the stars seven luminaries were conspicuous for their size and their movement among the heavenly host. Thirty never became a sacred number, although the moon was constantly symbolized by that number in documents, accomplished its lunations in that number of days, and, as heaven's indicator, measured time in periods of thirty days ; nor did three hundred and sixty-five become a heavenly number, although the sun-god completed his course in so many days, and accurately marked off the natural year. It seems to have been other associations connected with the number seven that rendered the seventh day and the seventh seventh day separate from all others in the Assyrian ritual, and that made the seventh day and the seventh month, perhaps, and the seventh year notable periods in Israel.

3

What other associations were there? Perhaps indications may be found in the ancient writings. Let us see.

According to the Babylonian narrative the flood, the fearful work of the gods, ceased on the seventh day. This fact is noteworthy because of its possible significance. Deity is at rest and man is relieved on the seventh day (Jensen).[1] But more than this. The Hebrew narrative, the strangely variant account given by Josephus, and the cuneiform story preserve, each in its own way, the recollection that the release from the ark and the sacrifice which the saved offered took place on a seventh day; the exit, according to the Hebrew narrative, being authorized by God on a seventh day long after the earth was dry. These facts also may be significant. Gracious relief is afforded to man by heaven, for which a thank-offering is made; afforded on the seventh day and, perhaps, as may appear later, expected to be afforded on that day. But yet more. In the Hebrew account of creation, in the periodic cessation of the manna, and in the law of the Sabbath the outstanding features are likewise divine rest and human relief on the recurring seventh day. Similar thoughts reappear in the feast on the first day of the seventh month, with its solemn rest and the special offering for a sweet savor unto the Lord (Lev. xxiii. 24, 25; Num. xxix. 1); in the consecration of the seventh year that the land might rest unto the Lord and recover its strength (Ex. xxiii. 11; Lev. xxv. 4); in the release of the seventh year which allowed the Hebrew bondman after six years of service to go forth free (Ex. xxi. 2; Deut. xv. 12 seq.); and in the jubilee, when, "seven times seven years" having been completed, liberty was proclaimed throughout the land (Lev. xxv. 8

---

[1] Such may also be the meaning of the Hebrew narrative. See chapter on the flood.

seq.). Each recurring seventh period of time is a season of rest, liberty, and joy. What do these things mean? An origin is needed for the belief that the seventh portion of time was a season of rest and good-will to man; a heavenly example calling for imitation on earth.

III

THE CREATION OF MAN

PRACTICALLY the universal belief of antiquity in regard to man's origin was that he was made of earth. It could not be otherwise, for the truth was evident to him that had eyes to see. Man's body moulders to dust after death. Plainly it is made of earth. The tales which would tell the story of man's creation differ, indeed, but the difference between the accounts which assume the intervention of a creator lies in the method of divine procedure.

In a review of the Semitic tradition of this event three narratives have special importance.

The Babylonian priest Berosus relates, in a passage already quoted, that Bel removed his head and other gods (or god) mixed the outflowing blood with earth and formed men; wherefore they are intelligent and partake of divine thought. Who the unnamed assistant of Bel was is not known. It has been conjectured that the deity was a goddess, namely Aruru, of whom it is related that, at a comparatively late date in human history, when a being was needed to counteract the influence of Izdubar, she washed her hands, plucked off clay, cast it to the ground, and made Eabani. This conjecture has received decided confirmation from a passage in the so-called " Non-Semitic Version of the Creation Story" where the two lines occur :

> "Bel made mankind,
> Aruru had made the seed of mankind with him." [1]

---

[1] The attempt to identify the god Ea with the nameless assistant of Bel is a failure so far as it is based on the claim that Ea " bears among other signifi-

The second of the three narratives to which attention is called comes from the Nile country. It is said to have been "of comparatively recent growth" (Wilkinson, Ancient Egyptians, vol. i., 1; cp. Brugsch, Steininschrift und Bibelwort, S. 14). It appears in its most elaborate form in a prayer and not in a formal account of the creation of man. A king is represented as approaching Chnum, the creator, and addressing the god thus: "I draw nigh to thee, holy architect, creator of the gods, builder of the egg, peerless one. At thy will the potter's wheel was brought unto thee, and on it thou didst model gods and men. Thou art the great, exalted god who in the beginning first formed this world (Brugsch, ibid., S. 15). The words of another inscription are more like the Hebrew transmission: "The great living god, who formed man and breathed the breath of life into his nose" (ibid., 16).

The third account has been transmitted by the Hebrews. "The Lord God formed man out of the dust of the ground, and breathed into his nostrils the breath of life, and man became a living soul."

cant names that of a potter" (Jensen, Kosmologie, S. 293). A better statement of the case is that the ideograms for god-potter are explained as a title of the god Ea. The name does not indicate that Ea did the work of a potter, but that he was the patron of the craft. It does not refer to Ea as being a potter, but as being god of the potter (II R., 58, No. 5, 57b, c.). The title falls to Ea because he is the god of wisdom, who knows everything and presides over every department of skill. On the tablet alluded to, after a series of titles referring to the dominion of Ea as "god of heaven and earth," " god of the creation," " god of the universe," there follows "god of wisdom." Because god of wisdom he is, as is particularized in the succeeding lines,

> god-potter = god Ea [as god] of the potter.
> god-smith = " " " " " " smith.
> god-singer = " " " " " " singer.
> god-lord-ships = " " " " " " sailor.

These titles do not mean that Ea wrought as a potter and as a blacksmith and as a sailor. They simply mean that Ea was the divine source of all skill and patron of the arts. The title god-potter therefore cannot be adduced as proof that the god who assisted Marduk in the creation of man was Ea.

Are these gross tales from Babylonia and Egypt to
serve as commentaries on the Hebrew narrative, showing that the conception of the Hebrew writer was gross
also; or does the Hebrew account represent a pure conception which underlies the other two narratives? Have
Babylonian and Egyptian originals been stripped of
everything repugnant to worshippers of the spiritual
God to yield the Hebrew account, or is it the pure tradition which during transmission by other people became
fantastically elaborated and corrupted?

To these queries it may be answered:

1. If the Babylonian, Hebrew, and Egyptian narratives
are rooted in one and the same tradition, but in process
of time grew apart, the differences are apt to be mainly
growth and the common elements to be the essential and
original or at least early features. Judged thus, the
potter's wheel is an amplification of the original tradition; for it is a feature peculiar to the Egyptian version
and is not essential to the process of shaping a human
figure out of clay. For like reasons the diverse statements, on the one hand that the Lord God breathed into
man's nostrils, and on the other that the creating god
mingled his blood with earth in order to form man, have
a common root in the tradition that God gave life to
man. The elements common to the three narratives are
that God formed man from the dust of the earth and
communicated life unto him. This is the germinal tradition, and it has been transmitted by the Hebrew in almost bald simplicity.

2. But let us shift the point of view. Apart from comparison with each other, considered in themselves indi-
vidually, the Egyptian and Assyrian tales are elabora-
tions. They are complex. The simple always precedes
the complex, the picture must have a motive. The subject of these narratives is man's origin. Experience or

revelation or both had taught that man's body is formed of the dust of the earth. The truth was also firmly grasped that God is the creator of all things. The resulting doctrine was that God created man, determining his shape and figure, forming him of the dust and giving to him life and breath. This is the basis of the story, the truth upon which man built. Its formal enunciation has no fascination, does not charm the imaginative mind, does not comport with Oriental mode of expression. Not content with a bald statement of the truth, fervent minds sought to lend life and color to the picture by portraying details and introducing explanations which a vivid imagination furnished. Man's body was made of earth. And the Egyptian worshipper, familiar with the sight of his fellow-countrymen shaping vessels of Nile clay on the indispensable wheel, conceives of the creator standing before the revolving disk and moulding the forms of gods and men out of earth.[1] The speculative Babylonian, knowing that the life is in the blood, wove into the accepted doctrine the theory that the creating god removed his head and had the outflowing blood mixed with earth in order that the man to be might live.[2] The Hebrew

[1] Brugsch's contention in his work on "Religion und Mythologie der alten Aegypter" is that the Egyptian mythology sprang from simple conceptions of nature, and that the doctrines were known and taught in practically their naked simplicity as well as in mythological garb during every period of Egyptian history. As bearing on the actual method which the creator was supposed to have pursued when he formed gods and men, it may be in place to quote two sentences from Egyptian writings : "He uttered his voice and the deities were," "The deities came into existence in accordance with the command of his mouth" (cited by Brugsch, ib., S. 98).

[2] That the story as told by Berosus is a modification of the original tradition appears also, we think, from the existence of a variant version in Babylonia which might mediate between the Hebrew and Egyptian accounts, did it not ascribe the work of creation to the sun-god. The tradition referred to is reflected in these words from a tablet : Marduk "made mankind, the merciful one with whom is power to make alive. May his word stand firm and not be forgotten in the mouth of the black-heads [i.e., men] whom his hands made" (AL[1] 42, AL[2] 80 and AL[3] 95, 15-18.).

historian, controlled by his lofty conception of God, refused to give flight to the imagination or to follow the grossness of heathen speculation. His account is nearer to the bald statement of the truth than either of its foreign counterparts. It is evidently the original stream of the tradition, colored—not discolored—by the nature of the channel through which it courses, but possessing still the character which it had at the fountain-head.

3. Let us shift the point of view again. Analogy is full of suggestiveness in this matter. Its testimony is not infallible, but it has value for purposes of corroboration and indication. It confirms the priority of the Hebrew form of the tradition; and going further, it emphasizes the Hebrew narrative as being, not a return to or towards the original, perhaps, but a survival of it. The theory of survival or of coexistence side by side with corrupted forms is demonstrable in the case of the Hebrew account of creation. It is certain, also, that the Hebrew narrative of the flood represents a purer transmission of the history of that event than do the extant Babylonian accounts. Analogy, accordingly, while it does not prove, yet favors the theory that the Hebrew narrative of man's creation is the stream of the original tradition, not clarified from impurities which had entered and rendered it unwholesome, but still flowing with waters which, though reflecting the color of their channel and banks, never lost their pristine sweetness and purity.

This cursory review of the three narratives has done more than bring to light their relation to the primitive tradition. It has laid bare the foundation of that tradition, and has shown that this foundation is not a heathen myth, but the universally accepted truth; the simple truth, afterwards distorted, that God made man's body of earth and bestowed the gift of life.

The next question that arises is whether the Hebrew

narrator meant to describe the method of divine procedure and to teach that God shaped a human form out
of the dust of the earth and with his mouth breathed
into the nostrils of this clay figure the breath of life ; or
whether, intending to teach, without bringing in or considering any extraneous ideas, simply that God, in creating man, determined his form, made him of earthy material, and gave him breath and life, used figurative
language which was current coin in the speech of plain
people.   For the expressions which are employed to describe the creation of man, even where they mirror
pictures, were current in the ordinary speech of the people.   The word *yatsar*, like its English equivalents "to
form, to fashion," has its special application to the arts.
It can describe the potter shaping the clay, and the
sculptor chiselling the stone, and the smith forging the
iron (Is. xlv. 9 ; xliv. 9, 12).   It would be the appropriate word to describe the work of moulding a human
figure out of the dust of the ground.   But it must not be
forgotten that the word has its general application.   Without calling up to the mind the image of potter, sculptor,
or smith, it is used to describe the Creator's work who
forms light and creates darkness, who formed summer
and winter, who formeth man in secret before birth, who
fashioneth our imperfect substance before it is brought
forth, who formeth the spirit of man within him (Is. xlv.
7 ; Ps. lxxiv. 17 ; Jer. i. 5 ; Ps. cxxxix. 16 ; Zech. xii. 1).
It is used also of God in calling a nation into being, as
when he created Jacob and formed Israel (Is. xliii. 1, 21).
It would be a fitting word to employ for the purpose of
describing the spiritual God willing and securing that
man's body be constituted of the dust of the ground.
This last phrase, too, "dust of the ground," must not be
arbitrarily and restrictedly understood ; it means com-
prehensively the material of the universe.   God is fur-

ther said to have breathed into man's nostrils the breath
of life. The language could aptly be used to express the
placing of the lips to the nostrils of clay and breathing
in vital breath until respiration was started and life began. But here again the use of language must be remembered. A mode of statement and a form of expression occur which, though capable of a realistic literal
interpretation, were current in the speech of ordinary
life in a sense quite devoid of realism. It need scarcely
be said that the words " God *breathed* into man's nostrils
the breath of life " may mean in Hebrew parlance merely
that God *caused the vital breath* to be in man's nostrils.
The breathing into the *nostrils*, moreover, does not necessarily imply the previous existence of an image of clay
with face and nose. Breath is felt in the nostrils and is
a sign of life. Breath in the nostrils is a current figure
for life. " All in whose nostrils was the breath of life "
perished in the flood. Man is ephemeral, his " breath is
in his nostrils." The statement that God breathed into
man's nostrils the breath of life may be the language of
a historian and mean simply that God imparted life to
man. The thought is summed up in the words : " And
man became a living soul." Very different, indeed, as
the sequel shows, from the great whales in the sea and
from the cattle and creeping things and beasts of the
earth, yet, like them, man was a living soul, *i.e.*, animate
(Gen. i. 20, 24 ; 1 Cor. xv. 45).

What, then, is the true interpretation ? What did the
Hebrew narrator himself mean ? The question, be it
observed, is not in what literary form the tradition
reached the Hebrew narrator. He may have quoted the
exact words of the Semitic transmission. A few Egyptians may have understood that God placed his lips to
the nostrils of clay. The uninstructed Israelite and the
careless reader may have interpreted the phraseology in

gross literalness. But that is not the question. The question is how the Hebrew narrator, whether he quoted or rewrote, understood; and whether he expected and intended his language to be pushed in the utmost literalness that it will bear, or to be taken in the current meaning of the terms. Surely he adopted the tradition in consonance with his conception of God. Literature which is incorporated with one's creed is adjusted to one's dominant belief. Even if amid the vicissitudes of transmission the truth as to man's origin accumulated about itself the rubbish of pagan speculation and reflected it in phraseology and passed thus burdened to Israel—a theory which, however, as already shown, is not favored by analogy—yet even so, as soon as the tradition was appropriated by the Hebrew narrator and transmitted to his countrymen, it lost for him and for them every thought and suggestion incompatible with his and their conception of God. It became naturalized in Israel. Henceforth it partook of the character of Israel's faith.

The narrator's conception of Jehovah is exalted and pure. Always, except occasionally during a theophany—e.g., in the garden (ii. 21, 22 (?), and iii. 8)—Jehovah operates in a distinctively divine manner. He accomplishes his purposes by act of will and control of nature. His outstretched hand, his look are but symbolical actions or figures of speech, not the efficient cause. They are anthropomorphisms which were to be expected, and they in nowise obscure the lofty conception of Jehovah. Nothing is too hard for him (Gen. xviii. 14), for he is the God and maker of heaven and earth (Gen. xxiv. 3; ii. 4). When he produces an effect in the visible world, he does it not as a man would. He wills, and the hidden processes of nature obey. He "planted a garden in Eden," not as a man would set out an orchard, but by "making trees to grow out of the ground" (Gen. ii. 8, 9). He remained in heaven, and yet discomfited the Egyptian host and took off their chariot-wheels (Ex. xiv. 24, 25). He uttered no word of command even, yet at his will in an instant the rod of Moses was a serpent and the hand was like snow with leprosy (Ex. iv. 2–7). He appeared to Moses and knew him face to face, yet this servant of God was profoundly aware that never, even in the most favored moment, had he beheld the essential glory of Jehovah, a glory which no man can look upon and live (Ex. xxxiii. 18–23). Such was the conception of Jehovah which the Hebrew historian who penned the description of man's creation out of the dust of the earth entertained in his mind and displayed in his writings. Surely he at least did not intend to teach that Jehovah God, when he formed man, stood as a potter at the wheel and slowly shaped the clay. According to the character ascribed, Jehovah God produced the result by act of will or by control of the forces of nature.

The same conception of the divine method of work was entertained, and the same high standard of interpretation established for the Church by him who placed the ancient traditions of the creation of the universe in general and the creation of man in particular side by side. He relates, indeed, that God made the luminaries, and put them in the firmament of heaven (Gen. i. 16, 17); but he does not mean that God fabricated them in his workshop and transported them to their places in the sky. He expressly states that God said: "Let there be lights in the firmament of heaven, and it was so " (vs. 14, 15; cp. also v. 6 with 7, 11 with 12, 20 with 21). He believed and taught that God's method of work differs from man's method, not in magnitude and magnificence merely, but radically in mode of operation. He spake and it was done, he commanded and it stood fast,

he willed and instantly or gradually, mediately or immediately, it finds accomplishment. At creation there was
no man to whom Jehovah God should manifest himself,
no occasion to veil his glory by standing at the potter's
wheel, no reason for working in other than his own sublime, divine manner, no appropriateness in forming
man's body otherwise than by act of will and the exercise of unseen power. He who placed the first and
second chapters of Genesis side by side, penning, it may
be, the very words of the old tradition concerning man's
creation, when judged by his own conception of God,
shared the view, it can scarcely be doubted, and fixed for
the church the interpretation alone valid and authorita-
tive that God formed man's body of earth and inspired it
with life by act of will and by the exercise of unseen
power.

The attitude of Scripture generally to the record of
man's creation deserves passing notice. In writings which
presuppose acquaintance with the second chapter of
Genesis, it is only outside of the Scriptures that the idea
is countenanced or taught that the Creator moulded earth
into a human figure when he would form man. Job and
Elihu have indeed been cited to the contrary. Job says:
"Thine hands have formed me and fashioned me, thou
hast fashioned me as clay; and wilt thou bring me into
dust again?" Elihu says: "The inspiration of the Almighty giveth men understanding." "The spirit of God
hath made me and the breath of the Almighty hath given
me life. I also have been nipped[1] from the clay" (x. 8
12; xxxii. 8; xxxiii. 4–6). Despite the strong language,
however, language strictly parallel to that used in the
second chapter of Genesis to describe the creation of
man, neither of these men thought that God had moulded
a piece of clay into human shape to form him. Each

[1] The same verb is used in the description of the formation of Eabani.

knew that he had been conceived in the womb and born (iii. 3, 11 ; x. 18 ; xxxi. 15). It may seem strange, but it is a fact, that the language which the writer of the second chapter of Genesis uses to describe man's creation is found in the mouth of these men when speaking of ordinary human conception and birth. And it may well be asked whether they did not believe that God in forming the first man wrought in a manner essentially like that which he adopts in bringing every man into the world.[1]

This chapter may find fitting conclusion in the thoughts regarding man which were shared by the Semites east and west and reflected in their traditions.

1. The apprehension of God as man's creator. This is somewhat remarkable; for in reference to the universe at large the Babylonian account of creation does not postulate the priority of God to matter. The gods of the pantheon, which are merely the heavenly bodies and other natural objects considered animistically, are said to come into existence. No act of creation is implied. But when the origin of man is concerned there is ever, as among the Hebrews, the clear apprehension that he is the creature and dependent of God.

2. The conception that man was created in the spiritual image of God. The Egyptian worshipper—who perhaps is not unjustly mentioned in the same breath with Semites when certain traditions are under discussion— the Egyptian worshipper thinks of men as formed by the same divine artificer in the same manner and on the same wheel with the created gods. The Babylonian scribe ex-

---

[1] Similarly, in a papyrus, language much like that used to describe the act of the Egyptian god in creating man is employed of the ordinary divine agency experienced by every man, where none but a figurative interpretation seems to be possible. The papyrus dates from the nineteenth dynasty, that of the Pharaohs of the oppression and exodus. Phtah is hailed as the fashioner of men, the former of the gods, the lord of life who opens the throat and affords breath to the noses of all (Brugsch, Religion u. Mythologie, S. 512 f.).

pressed the same thought when he records that the blood of the creating god entered into the composition of men so that they are intelligent and partake of divine thought. The doctrine is enunciated in the first chapter of Genesis in the words, " God created man in his own image, in the likeness of God created he them."

3. The sense of the gulf between man and beast. The feeling manifests itself in the Babylonian narrative in the passage already cited. It is embodied in the belief entertained by the Israelites that at death the spirit of the beast goeth downward, but the spirit of man goeth upward. It is beautifully exhibited in the picture of Adam scanning the animals as they come before him, distinguishing them by names from each other and from himself until, having separated and bounded off bird and beast, he discovers that he is alone. He finds none of his own kind. He has no spiritual likeness and no companionship with the beasts about him.

IV

THE HELP MEET FOR MAN

THE Semitic tradition of the creation of woman cannot be studied with satisfaction as yet. The materials are too scanty, for no parallel to the Hebrew narrative has been found. Professor Sayce, it is true, believes that he has discovered a passage in one of the Assyro-Babylonian magical texts which "indicates that a similar view as to the creation of the woman from the man prevailed in Babylonia to that which we read of in the book of Genesis. In W. A. I., iv. 1., i. 36, 37, it is said of the seven evil spirits: 'The woman from the loins of the man they bring forth,' in conformity with the Semitic belief which derived the woman from the man" (Hibbert Lectures, 1887, p. 395, note). But suppose that to the words quoted from the tablet by the distinguished professor there be added, in his own translation elsewhere given (ibid., 451, l. 17, 18), the line that follows in the original. The statement of the text then is

"The woman from the loins of the man they bring forth,
The child from the knees of the man they cause to issue."

The passage as rendered describes the malicious pranks of demons who sometimes in their malevolence bring forth a woman out of the loins of a man, at other times take a child out of his knee. There is no reference at all to the creation of woman, no evidence that a similar view prevailed in Babylonia to that which is taught in the book of Genesis.

The statement that opinion as to the creation of

woman was similar in Babylonia and Palestine is, furthermore, based on a questionable translation. The meaning
of the word rendered "loins" is not certain. The ideogram which corresponds to it in the accompanying Babylonian text represents several vocables, one of which
means "foundation" and another denotes a part of the
body of man and beast. This latter word, which is commonly understood to mean loins or buttocks or legs
(AL³ Tfl. 128), may accordingly be a synonym of the word
used in the Assyrian text which is quoted by Professor
Sayce. If so, it may be correct to render the word of the
text either, with Professor Sayce, by loins, or else by buttocks or legs. This latitude of meaning should be borne
in mind when the inscription is interpreted and should
prevent the unqualified assertion from being made that
the passage reflects the Hebrew belief.

There is yet other objection to seeing in the passage
a reflection of the Hebrew belief as to the creation of
woman. The text as a whole is not altogether free from
obscurity, but the subject of the story seems to be not
the malicious pranks of demons, but rather the impossi-
bility of escape from their pursuit.[1] Quoted more largely,
the passage is as follows :

"From house to house they pass.
As for them, the door does not restrain them,
The lock does not turn them ;
In at the door like a snake they go,
In at the threshold like the wind they blow ;
A woman [who is] at the loins (?) of a man they lead away,
A child [who is] at the knee of a man they draw forth,
A noble [who is] in the house of his kindred they drive out.
They are the scourging voice who behind a man go."

The Hebrew narrative of the provision of a help meet
for man has been held by not a few readers to be a par-

---

[1] The correctness of this latter view is corroborated by IV R., 27, No. 5, especially l. 7–13.

4

able ; as though its author intended to give a poetical or
symbolical exhibition of the truth, rather than to relate
an actual occurrence.   There is no inherent objection to
this view.   But since some of these early narratives are
clearly the tradition of events and the account of facts,
the narrative of the provision of a companion for man
must be so regarded until, perchance, discovery among
Assyro-Babylonian tablets reveals in unmistakable manner that the narrative is intentionally a poetic composition.

Regarded, then, as intended to be the account of an
event, the Hebrew narrative represents the man as sunk
in deep sleep and yet as seeing what occurs during the
stupor, for on awakening he recognizes the woman who is
brought to him as her who had been taken out of him.
The narrative thus portrays man either as lying in a
trance, feeling nothing yet conscious of what was taking
place ; or as beholding a vision, in which the scene was
apparent only, not real.

Strong reasons exist for understanding the intent of
the tradition to be that the action seen during sleep was
real and that woman was formed in the manner described.   The place assigned to the account suggests
this ; the creation of man has been described, it is appropriate for information to be next given as to woman's
origin.   The absence elsewhere of a particular account
of how woman was made is corroboration.   It is true
that in the preceding chapter there is the record that
God created man male and female.   But that account is
general.   Should there not be, as of the creation of man,
so also of the creation of woman, a particular account ?
The superscription of the narrative countenances the
indications which arise from the place occupied by the
account : "It is not good that man should be alone."
These words are more like the introduction to an in-

tended account of woman's creation, than merely of her
presentation to man amidst a halo of wholesome truth.
The impression, furthermore, made by the recital upon
readers, learned and unlearned, has, with few exceptions,
ever been that the narrator means to tell how woman
was made. These considerations raise the strong presumption that in the intent of the tradition the action
seen during sleep was a reality.

Nevertheless the psychological features are distinctly
those of a vision. It was the divine purpose that man
should not be alone; God determined to make a suitable
help for man. And this is what took place, according
to the tradition, as the divine purpose was about to be
realized in human experience. When man was created,
he was allowed to come in contact with the beasts and
birds which God had made. As they came under his
observation, he noted their cries and their traits and
their habits and gave to each a fitting name. But as he
observed them thus attentively, he noted also that they
were male and female, that they were of different kinds,
that all of one kind associated by themselves and found
joyous companionship together; but that nowhere did
he, the man, meet with one of his own kind; that, unlike
the other living creatures, there was no female his counterpart; that for him there was no companion; that there
was none about him that betrayed knowledge of God or
sense of obligation or perception of relationship to the
world around; that he was alone and solitary and help-
less on earth. Yearning was awakened in him for companionship, and the kind of being suitable for him was
clearly suggested to his mind. Then the Lord God
caused a deep sleep to fall upon him, and he slept;
and he saw and lo! the Lord God took one of his ribs
and closed up the flesh instead thereof; and the rib,
which the Lord God took from man, made he a woman.

And the Lord God brought the woman seen during the deep sleep to the man when he awoke, and Adam recognizing her said: "This is now bone of my bone and flesh of my flesh."

If this was a vision—and the Greek translators so understood, for they rendered the word for deep sleep in this passage and in another presently to be mentioned by ecstasy [1]—if this was a vision, it resembles the vision of Abraham at Hebron in the literary form in which it is narrated (Gen. xv. 12–18), and in its psychology that of Peter at Joppa. In literary form it is like the vision of Abraham, for the subjective is related as objective. "When the sun was going down, a deep sleep fell upon Abram and the Lord said to him: 'Know of a surety that thy seed shall be a stranger in a land that is not theirs.' And when the sun went down, and it was dark, behold a smoking furnace and a burning lamp that passed between those pieces." It is like the vision which Peter saw at Joppa in the providential preparation of the mind for a phantasm which should convey truth. Peter hungered exceedingly, fell into a stupor, saw a vision of food let down from heaven in a sheet, heard a command to eat, refused because the meats were ceremonially unclean, perceived a voice saying: "What God hath cleansed call not thou common." Then while Peter doubted in himself what this vision which he had seen should mean, behold there were three men already come unto the house where he was, desiring him to visit and teach a gentile (Acts x. 9–17; xi. 11, 12). In like manner the thoughts of Adam were turned powerfully to the absolute lack of companionship for him among birds and beasts, his attention was directed to the twofold character of the animals which made their lairs and built their nests together and wrought in mutual helpfulness,

[1] Such is also Bishop Ellicott's opinion.

and his mind was made to dwell on his solitude. Then deep sleep fell upon him, and he saw one of his ribs taken out by the Lord God, the place closed up with flesh, and a woman formed. He awoke. Immediately, or after a time, the woman whom he had seen in his sleep is brought unto him, and, recognizing her, he exclaims: "This is now bone of my bone and flesh of my flesh; she shall be called woman, because she was taken out of man."

If this was a vision, it was the method employed by God to reveal to man those truths regarding woman upon which the moral relations rest. In a symbolic manner man is taught that woman is one blood with him, that she equally with him is the handiwork of God, that she was created for the man, was committed unto him by God, and has her place by inherent right at man's side as help and companion.

It may be that like Paul, who knew not whether he was in the body or out of the body, the seer of this vision was ignorant whether the event was subjective or objective. He transmitted it just as it occurred, without note or comment, as a revelation of God which inculcated truth even if in a symbolic manner.

There is no doubt as to which interpretation is acceptable to the spirit of modern thought. The appeal, however, must not be solely to modern thought when a tradition of hoar antiquity is to be interpreted. The main question is what the originators and early transmitters of the tradition intended to teach. A relevant remark is that it is distinctly and decidedly in accord with old Babylonian tradition, as well as with biblical history, for divine revelation to be made by symbolic dreams.

One word may be allowed in conclusion regarding a detail of the narrative. The Hebrew statement that woman was called 'ishshâh because she was taken from '*ish*, man, has been severely criticised. The charge is made that a false popular etymology is advanced, and that the Hebrew writer erroneously regarded '*ishshâh* as the grammatical feminine of '*ish*. The objection is raised unhappily, for the question of etymology is not involved in the narrative. The derivation of the word '*ishshâh* is not the subject under discussion by the Hebrew writer, and has no bearing on the authenticity of the record. The narrative of the divine provision of a help meet for man is, doubtless, like its companions, a hoary tradition which was handed down from Semitic ancestors to the Israelites, and as the Hebrew language took shape was translated into the new dialect. The words '*ish* and '*ishshâh* render into Hebrew the corresponding foreign words of the tradition. The Hebrew narrator no more asserts that '*ishshâh* is derived from the same root as '*ish* than did the English scholars offer an etymology for the word woman when in translating the Scriptures they rendered " she shall be called woman because she was taken out of man."

V

THE SITE OF THE GARDEN OF EDEN

"A RIVER went out of Eden to water the garden; and from thence it was parted and became four heads" (Gen. ii. 10). These words are understood by Friedrich Delitzsch to mean that the stream which came from Eden parted after leaving the garden and flowed onward through four channels. Glaser, on the other hand, understands the words to mean that the stream divided into its own four heads; each head being itself a river, as is expressly stated (vs. 13, 14). Glaser, indeed, thinks that the confluence of these tributaries was below the garden, Paradise being situated on some one of them; but it is better perhaps to modify his theory so far as to understand that the stream which came from Eden and watered the garden, "from that point," not necessarily after flowing through the garden, but from that locality, divided as one followed it toward its source and became four heads. According to one interpretation the river of Eden divided to embrace island countries in its onward flow, or to form a delta and seek the sea by various mouths as the Nile does; according to the other conception the great stream, as it was followed upward, was found to divide into four heads, as the Indus separates and has for its head-waters the five rivers of the Punjaub, and as the Mississippi parts into the Red River, the Arkansas, the Ohio, the Missouri and the upper stream of its own name. The question will be decided if the four rivers named can be discovered. It will then be seen whether they flow out of a single stream as so many mouths, or whether, as so many heads, they flow together and constitute a single stream.

Friedrich Delitzsch holds that the river which " went out of Eden to water the garden " is the Euphrates. Entering the alluvial plain at a higher level and continuing to flow for some distance at greater altitude than the Tigris, the Euphrates, without the aid of its sister stream, fed the numerous canals which irrigated the intervening country as far south as Babylon, and was the one stream which watered the garden. Below Babylon its abundant waters gathered themselves into four great water-courses. The first of these streams is the western branch of the Euphrates, the celebrated canal Pallakopas, which was doubtless an old natural channel converted by man into a canal. The second is the eastern branch of the Euphrates, which, after flowing through the entire central part of Babylonia, rejoined the main channel. The third is the Tigris, which, after receiving water from the Euphrates through the canals which irrigated the garden, again flowed onward an independent stream. The fourth is the Euphrates, which, remarkably enough, not only has been assigned the last place in the narration, but has been left without description; an omission due certainly not to the fact that the river was known to every Hebrew—for that was also the case with the Tigris—but to its being the chief stream, the one that watered the garden, the true river of Paradise. The eastern branch of the Euphrates is probably meant by the 'Gugân dê of the inscriptions, approximately Gihon; and since the Kashshu from the mountains had settled in Babylonia, this branch of the great river could be described as compassing the whole land of Cush. The Pishon, which has been identified with the western branch of the Euphrates, compassed the land of Havilah : a name which,

judging from Gen. x. 29, xxv. 18; 1 Sam. xv. 7, denoted
some portion of the Syrian desert—a part of which [a
small district in the west] is still known as Ard el-chálàt
—or, more particularly, designated the territory which
bordered on Babylonia and extended to the Persian
Gulf. As gold, bdellium, and shoham stone were produced in Babylonia, they were doubtless products of the
adjacent region across the Euphrates as well; that is,
ex hypothese, of Havilah, where, according to the Hebrew
narrator, they were found. It is stated further that the
stream which watered the garden came out of Eden. Now
the Assyrian word *êdinu* means a plain; and the alluvial
lowlands at the head of the Persian Gulf and the river
bottoms for a considerable distance northward are
known at this day as "the depression," in contrast with
the higher desert plateau. It is therefore quite conceivable that *êdinu*, *i.e.*, Eden, denotes this portion of Mesopotamia; the more so because the nomadic tribes who
roamed through this very region were called by the Assyrians *tsâbê êdini*, "the people of the plain."

Such, in brief, is the admirably wrought-out theory of
Friedrich Delitzsch. Its weakness lies first in the mul-
titude of unsupported conjectures upon which the identifications rest. Gihon is a common appellative for any
rushing stream, and hence the name, even if actually
borne by a Babylonian canal, does not prove that particular watercourse to be the river which is referred to
in the description of Eden. Pishon is assumed to have
been the ancient name of the Pallakopas, and this assumption makes necessary the further supposition that
the land of Havilah, which was surrounded by the river
Pishon, reached to the bank of the Euphrates, a geographical extension not supported by the biblical passages relied upon. A second weakness appears in the
improbability that gold and shoham stone, which are

stated by the Hebrew writer to have been obtained in
Havilah, were products of the alluvial soil of Babylonia.
The evidence that Babylonia was a gold-producing country is found in a single passage. It is recorded that
Merodach-baladan, who reigned in southern Babylonia,
brought as tribute to Tiglath-pileser, among other costly
gifts, " gold, the dust of his land, in great quantity." The
dust of southern Babylonia was thus gold or contained
gold. But is this conclusion warranted? Was the gold
found in the alluvium at the mouth of the two rivers?
What searcher after the precious metal ever found it
there? The hereditary kingdom of Merodach-baladan
was, indeed, on the northern shore of the gulf; but is
not the citation of this passage in proof that Babylonia
produced the gold an assumption that the boundaries
of Merodach-baladan's realm were confined to the alluvial plain at the mouth of the two rivers and did not,
at least during his reign, include the extensive region to
the southwest, where gold is known to have been found?
As to the shoham stone, when it is mentioned as a product of Melucha, proof must be furnished that the country intended is not the distant Melucha from which the
early kings of Babylonia imported gold and costly wood.

Glaser bases a theory on other identifications. He
argues from the biblical references that Havilah was situated in the interior of Arabia, and corresponded to the
district of Yemama with its extensions to the northwest
and southwest (Skizze der Geschichte und Geographie
Arabiens, S. 323–326). This land was unquestionably a
gold-producing region, and with the adjacent territory
was almost the exclusive source of gold supply for the
nations of antiquity. In this region precious stones also
were obtained; and bdellium, which is commonly understood to be the article referred to by the Hebrew writer
under the name of *b'dôlach*. This region is drained by a

great wady, of which one of the forks was known to the
early Arabian geographers as the Faisân, *i.e.*, in Hebrew
Pêshôn. The waters of the wady fail, however, to reach
the gulf, a peculiarity of many Arabian rivers, and can
only be traced by the character of the vegetation (S.
342–347). In central and eastern Arabia, more definitely in Jebel Shamar and the adjacent country to the
south and east as far as the Persian Gulf, Cushites dwelt
at one period of history as they were migrating from
Elam to Abyssinia, thereby causing the country to be
known for a time as the land of Cush (S. 338 and 355,
and cp. Gen. x. 7) ; and the wady Rumma, which gathers
the waters of this region and conducts them toward the
Persian Gulf, was known in olden time as Djaichân, or,
as the Hebrews would render it, Gêchôn, *i.e.*, Gihon (S.
342 and 355).

Glaser accordingly interprets the Hebrew writer as
meaning that below the garden of Eden was a place
where four rivers united. Two of these were the Tigris
and the Euphrates ; the others were the wady Pishon,
which drains a part of central Arabia, and the wady
Rumma, formerly Gihon, which carries off the waters of
the neighboring region on the north. The garden, however, cannot be accurately located, he thinks, even if the
uniting-place of the four rivers were fully known, because we do not know on which of the four rivers
Paradise was situated. We may assume that the biblical author conceived of the garden as being immediately above the confluence of the four rivers. This place
must be sought in the neighborhood of Bosra (S. 320–
322).

The fatal point at which the theory of Glaser breaks is
his identification of the Gihon with the wady er-Rumma.
This identification rests upon a mistake. The poet, upon
whom Glaser relies, does not refer to a river of Arabia,

when he mentions the Gihon, but to the Pyramus in Cilicia (Noeldeke, ZDMG., 44, 4, 1890, pp. 699–700).

Friedrich Delitzsch brought forward proof to show that Cush is, in the first instance, practically the same as Elam. This fact Fritz Hommel introduces as a modification of Glaser's theory. He accepts the identification of Havilah with the mountain district of Yemama in Arabia. In regard to the land of Cush, he claims that it becomes more and more probable that Elam as a whole—not excepting the region north of it, known to the classic Greek writers and the inscriptions of the later Assyrian kings as the country of the Cossæans—was called Kash in earlier times. According to this, our Kush (originally Kôsh, derived from Kâsh) is the same as Elam; and the Gihon is the Kherkhah, which rises in the Cossæan mountains, flows past Susa, and now empties into the Tigris below its union with the Euphrates, but which in ancient times perhaps found an outlet directly into the Persian Gulf. South Babylonia is the neighborhood in which in the earliest times the Babylonians (or the Sumerians), and after them the Hebrews, located Paradise " (Sunday-School Times, December 5, 1891).

Despite these scholarly investigations, it can scarcely be said that the location of the garden has been finally determined. Research has, however, been rich in results; and facts have been ascertained and data obtained which bid fair to enter into the final solution of the problem. These factors are:

1. Mesopotamia was known in whole or in part as êdinu.

2. Havilah was a district in the eastern part of the Arabian peninsula. In this neighborhood is found the mountainous region now known as Yemama, a land of gold and aromatic gums and drained by a wady which, in a part of its course at least, went by the name of Pê-

shôn. Whether the waters of this wady ever reached the gulf remains, however, a question.

3. The name Cush, or its equivalent, belonged, with greater or less extension, to the region of mountain and tableland which lies to the east and northeast of Babylonia.[1]

4. The Persian Gulf was called a river, the nâr marrâtu. So to-day the estuary which embraces Manhattan Island is called a river. As the nâr marrâtu lay partly within the plain and received a large proportion of its waters from Mesopotamia, it could be regarded as coming out of, rather than as extending into, the plain êdinu. Into this "river" the Tigris and Euphrates, and rivers of Elam, and perhaps wadies of Arabia, discharged their waters.

If the facts which have been stated shall eventually be found to bear upon the site of the garden of Eden, it will be seen that the four rivers are enumerated, in the Hebrew description, in geographical order. The most southern, according to these data, was the Pishon, and

---

[1] The relation between the names *Kashshû*, κοσσᾶιοι, and κίσσιοι, is still in dispute. It is known that in the time of Sennacherib the Kashshû occupied a district "between Assyria and Elam on the borders of Media;" that the κοσσᾶιοι were found in the valleys of the Zagros Mountains on the borders of Media; and that in the days of Darius the Great and his successors κισσίη was the country in which Susa was situated. Whether these names represent unrelated peoples, or different branches of the same folk, is beyond our present purpose to inquire.

Kashshû	= κοσσᾶιοι,	but not	κίσσιοι,	Halévy, ZA., vol. iv., 208.
"	= "	uncertain as to	"	Schrader, KGF., 176 seq.
"	= κίσσιοι,	but not	κοσσᾶιοι,	Oppert, ZA., vol. iii., 421 seq.
				Lehmann, ibid., vii., 328 seq.
"	= "	and	"	Delitzsch, Paradies, S. 54, unten;
				Tiele, Geschichte, S. 70 oben.
"	= κοσσᾶιοι,			Noeldeke, N.G.G W., 1874, St. 8, S. 178 seq.

Whatever relation these words bear to each other, one or more names hovered about the high land on the east and northeast of Babylonia, which could be reproduced in Hebrew כוּשׁ, just as the Hebrews made Kûsh out of *Kash*, *Kaish*, *Kesh*, *Kish*, the names by which Ethiopia was known to the Egyptians.

drained the land of Havilah; the next, on the north, flowing in from the east, came from the mountain land of Cush ; the next in order to the north was the Tigris; and the most northern and the main stream was the Euphrates.

THE SO-CALLED ADAM AND EVE CYLINDER.

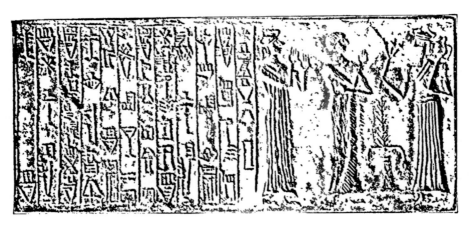

SEAL OF DUNGI, KING OF UR.

Showing the head-dress of a god, a priest and a worshipper. An act of worship is in progress.

SEAL WITH A SERPENT AND OTHER EMBLEMS.

A god is receiving adoration.

VI

THE TEMPTATION OF MAN

In the Babylonian and Oriental Record for October, 1890, and again in the Christian Commonwealth, Mr. W. St. C. Boscawen has published what he believes to be the Chaldean tradition of the fall of man. He says: "In one of the Creation tablets, perhaps the third of the series, there occurs near the end a most remarkable passage.

The great gods, all of them the foretellers of fate,
Entered and in a deadly manner the god Sar was filled [with anger].
Wickedness one with another in assembly makes.
The word was established in the garden of the gods.
They had eaten the *asnan* fruit, they had broken . . .
Its juice they sucked . . . .
The sweet juice which in drinking crushes the body.
Great is their sin . . . in exalting [themselves].
To Merodach their redeemer he has appointed the destiny.

It is clearly to be seen," continues Mr. Boscawen, "that here, unfortunately in a somewhat mutilated form, we have a most important tradition. It has the important elements common to the Hebrew tradition of the anger of the god, here the god Sar, the god of 'the hosts of heaven,' the 'Lord of Hosts,' who punishes with death; the eating of the fruit of the asnan tree, the sin; and the appointment of Merodach to be the redeemer of those who had sinned.

"There are several points of special interest in this

text. In the first place, the asnan tree is most remarkable. It is a word which means double parallel, and evidently explains the reason why the sacred tree on the Assyrian monuments is represented with two stalks; and also, I think, explains the confusion between the two trees in the Hebrew Genesis, the tree of life and the tree of knowledge of good and evil. . . . Still more important is the word at the end of the last line but one, *itellu* 'they exalted themselves,' when we consider it in connection with the expression in the Bible, 'Behold, man is become as one of us to know good and evil.' I now come to the most important point of all, and one fortunately on which there can be no doubt on the ground of mutilation of text. 'To Merodach their redeemer he appointed the destiny.' Here the expression admits of no other translation, it occurs in many inscriptions with the meaning of 'restorer of satisfaction,' as in the case of obtaining satisfaction for war or rebellion. . . . We have, therefore, in this a clear indication of the Messianic office of Merodach according to the Babylonian teaching. We must remember also that in the great tablet of the War in Heaven, it is Merodach who slays the serpent and crushes the brain of the creature—bruising his head. I venture, therefore, with every confidence to say that in this little but priceless fragment we have clear indications that a story of the fall, very closely resembling in detail that of Genesis iii., was current in Babylonia at an early period."

These articles by Mr. Boscawen have been widely copied. The scholarship of their learned author has been relied upon for the essential accuracy of the translation. In this instance, however, the work of Mr. Boscawen is faulty. According to the context and to a comparison with the ninth line of the text, the characteristic and determining phrase translated " in the garden of the gods " should be rendered "at a feast." The asnan tree, in which reference is seen to the tree of knowledge of good and evil and on the ground of which the charge of confusion is brought against the Hebrew narrative, was probably not a tree at all, but wheat or some other grain (Zimmern, Busspsalmen, S. 99; Jensen, Kosmologie, S. 279). The eating of the asnan fruit is an act of the gods themselves and not of man; and it is described, not as a sin, but as one of the pleasures of the repast. The destiny appointed for Marduk is not that of redeemer, but of avenger; and he is not sent forth in behalf of sinners, but to avenge the gods who had been sinned against. In fact the passage has no reference at all to the garden of Eden and the fall of man. It occurs in the Creation tablets after Marduk has offered to go forth against Tiamat as avenger of the gods and before he has been commissioned for the conflict. It tells how the gods who determine destiny entered [perhaps into assembly for consultation], celebrated a feast together, appointed the destiny for Marduk, set him in the princely chamber and, when he had acquiesced in their investiture of him with regal authority, hailed him as now numbered among the great gods and as their authorized avenger.

No trace of an Assyrian or Babylonian parallel to the Hebrew narrative of the temptation has yet come to light, unless it exist in the well-known intaglio. On this celebrated cylinder seal a tree is engraved; beneath the boughs of foliage two bunches of fruit hang from the trunk on long naked stems; on each side of the tree a being, in form human, is seated facing the tree and extending the hand as though to grasp the fruit; in the rear of one of the figures, or rather between the backs of the two (for the engraving encircles the cylinder), a serpent is seen erect as though standing. The picture at once strikes the beholder as a representation of the

5

temptation. All the elements of the narrative seem to be present. Lenormant asserts that "it does not lend itself to any other interpretation" (Les origines de l'histoire, p. 91), and Delitzsch goes so far as to declare that it is the fall (Paradies, S. 90).

The reference to the temptation is, however, problematical. Of course the fact that the figures are robed, wear coverings on the head, and sit on chairs does not militate against their being intended to represent Adam and Eve. It would only be another instance of the corruption to which traditions were subjected in Babylonia, and another example of the superiority of the Hebrew transmission. Primitive man did not weave cloth and manufacture stools; his first raiment was the skin of beasts. But still the reference of the picture to the fall of man is doubtful. Schrader has always maintained that an allusion to the fall cannot be proved; and he points out that a specific feature of the narrative, namely, that the woman gave the fruit to the man, is not indicated (KAT²., S. 37). The workmanship of the seal is rude; so rude indeed that it is not clear whether one of the figures is intended for a woman, or whether both are meant for men. Sayce says that "the two figures seem both to be males" (Smith, Chaldean Account of Genesis, ed. Sayce, p. 89). Menant also believes them to be men (Glyptique orientale, Iᵉ P., p. 189 seq.). Their raiment affords no aid in determining their sex; for each wears a plain robe which reaches to the ankles. Nor does the different head-gear distinguish them as man and woman, as Delitzsch asserts that it does (Paradies, S. 90). In Assyrian and Babylonian art the horned head-dress is found sometimes on the head of a god, sometimes on the head of a sacred attendant, sometimes on both; and the hat or turban is sometimes worn by the god, and sometimes by the worshipper. Nor does the presence of the serpent decide the meaning of the scene. It may have been introduced for the purpose of ornament, or the better to distinguish this signet from others, and not as significant of the temptation. Animals of various kinds are of common occurrence on the seals for such purposes. A snake is figured in the field of the third seal shown on the page of illustrations at the beginning of this chapter, a seal which represents the adoration of a god and strikingly resembles the so-called Adam and Eve cylinder in several particulars; and on the seal reproduced in the accompanying cut, in which events in the career of Izdubar are depicted, the serpent and other emblems not essential to the story are introduced. While, therefore, it is not impossible that the engraving on the so-called Adam and Eve seal is a representation of the temptation, yet it is equally, if not more, probable that it depicts a god receiving adoration from a priest or other worshipper.

IZDUBAR AND THE BULL, EABANI AND A LION.

A serpent separates the two groups; in the field are also a
scorpion and a bird.

VII

THE SERPENT OF THE TEMPTATION

THE thought came to George Smith, as it has come to
every reader of Babylonian tradition since, that there
may be some connection between the dragon of the Chaldean creation story and the serpent of Genesis. The
formidable Tiamat, commonly called a dragon because
terrible by nature and represented as a composite monster, was the disturber of order and the enemy of the
gods. The serpent of the book of Genesis sought to
undo the work of God by seducing man to rebel against
his maker. The idea of some connection between these
two foes of good is alluring, but on reflection it does
not seem probable.

The question is not whether the Chaldean story of
the dragon ever furnished the prophets of Israel with imagery to set forth their thought. Sublime literature may
legitimately borrow the fancies of fable and appropriate
them to its own use. The question is whether the conception of the dragon foe of Marduk and the serpent
tempter of man have community of origin : whether, if
traced back far enough, they would be found to merge
into the same account or, if not that, whether one would
be found to have suggested the figure of the other. It is
this which on reflection does not seem probable.

The accounts of the conflict of Marduk with Tiamat
and of the temptation of man are not counterparts. They
narrate entirely different events. So much is clear. But
although the events are entirely different, the same evil

being might be a prominent participant in both. The two narratives might relate to different episodes in the career of the same incarnate agent of evil.

Hebrew literature does not countenance such a theory, despite the effort that has been made to prove that it does. The argument has been advanced that in Job, in the Psalms and in Isaiah there are allusions to the Babylonian dragon-myth. Sound exegesis casts doubt upon the correctness of this allegation in most, if not all, instances; but it is not necessary to discuss that question here. The more plausible it can be made that "the origin of Rahab and Leviathan is to be found in that of Tiamat" (PAOS., vol. xv. 25), the clearer does it become that the serpent of the temptation and the monster of the myth were sharply defined and distinct from each other in the Hebrew mind. In the book of Enoch, further, "the serpent whose name is Tabaet" (= Tiamat, suggests Barton, PAOS., vol. xv. 20 seq.) is distinguished from the wicked angel Gadrel who descended to earth and seduced Eve. It is not until the Christian era, long after the exile, centuries after the story of Bel and the dragon had become familiar to the Jews, that there is any semblance of combining striking elements of the two narratives. It has been conjectured that the seer of Patmos had the story of Tiamat in mind and employed its imagery when he drew his great picture of the dragon, "the old serpent, he that is called the devil and Satan." Of course, the assumption that Tiamat was in the thought of the poet, rather than the innumerable dragons of which men have dreamed, is groundless; but it may pass unchallenged. Let its validity be granted. With the fervid imagination of the poet, John the divine seized upon the salient features of the two arch-enemies, and blended the borrowed characteristics in a new creation of his inspired genius. But in doing so he is far from identifying the two agents of evil. The devil which John describes is not the Tiamat of the Babylonian myth, even though he embodies in Satan certain attributes of the she-monster.

The art and literature of Babylonia, at present available, are equally at variance with the theory that Tiamat's conflict with Marduk and the serpent's seduction of the woman are but different episodes in the career of the same evil being. A cylinder seal, of which a sketch is presented herewith, has been cited to the contrary, as affording the connecting link between the tempter-serpent and the monster Tiamat. The seal was discovered by Dr. William Hayes Ward in the possession of the

late Hon. S. Wells Williams. "It represents," to quote Dr. Ward's detailed explanation, "a fleeing serpent, with its head turned back toward a deity, who is swiftly pursuing it, and who smites it with a weapon. The other figures in the seal have no relation to the pursuit of the serpent by the god. They are put in by the engraver simply to fill up the space, although all separately significant, no doubt. The small kneeling figure probably represents the owner of the seal. The two other figures behind the god represent no recognizable deities, and may be meant for priests. Filling up the smaller spaces are the female emblem κτείς, six planets, or perhaps stars of the Pleiades, and two smaller branches, which it would be hazardous to regard as representing the two trees of the garden of Eden" (Bibliotheca Sacra, 1881, p. 224).

To understand the significance of this seal, it must
be compared with others. For this purpose Dr. Ward
selects a cylinder made familiar
by George Smith. "It will be
seen," says Dr. Ward, "that this
is very much like Dr. Williams'
cylinder. The dragon, which
corresponds with the serpent in

the latter, is in the attitude of retreat, and turns its head
back toward its pursuer, who is running rapidly and who
shoots it with an arrow. The figure of the priest is the
same (reversed), and of the kneeling owner, as also the
representation of the minor accessories, the stars and
the κτείς, although the winged circle, emblem of the supreme power, replaces the crescent of the moon-god.
There is also a figure of a winged monster represented
under the feet of Bel, for which there was not room on
Dr. Williams' cylinder, but where an indistinct line or
two indicates that it was in the mind of the engraver.
It was very likely an attendant of the Dragon, or possibly of Bel. . . . We may, then, regard this new seal
of Dr. Williams as certainly representing the conflict of
Bel and the Dragon, the dragon being figured as a serpent."

Dr. Ward may be followed thus far, but no farther.
No intermediate story is implied by the engraving on
the seal, as he presently supposes. The scene depicted
on the cylinder does not exhibit a tradition in which
"the demiurge Bel-Merodach attacks and punishes the
serpent by bruising its head." It has no likeness to the
narrative in Genesis, in which the serpent is not slain
by God, as pictured on the seal, but is condemned to go
on its belly, eat dust, and be bruised on the head by the
seed of the woman. There is no reason to believe that
the cylinder tells any other story than the traditional
conflict of Marduk and Tiamat. The scene is obviously

the same as that depicted on the other seal, which is unquestionably the familiar tale. The difference is one of detail only; the beast, instead of being the conventional dragon, has the body and tail of a serpent. But its head is delineated with the familiar features of the dragon; it has the two ears, the proboscis-like projection in front, the spines on the neck. It has the same sex as the dragon, if any conclusion may be drawn from the diamond or κτείς, which here, as frequently on other cylinders, is placed near it. And it appears to be attacked through the mouth, as was the great she-monster of the deep in the story as told by the tablets, and as depicted on the companion seal. The huge, snake-like creature is one of the variant forms which the dread primeval ocean assumed in imagination.[1] Indeed the form of the body is perhaps an adaptation of the conventional mode of depicting water, and serves to more positively identify the monster as typical of the sea. Water is thus represented under a boat on the cylinder reproduced in the next chapter, and there, as here, forms part of the body of a composite creature. The picture on the Williams' seal affords no evidence of a story essentially different from the current myth. We are still dealing with the conflict of Marduk and Tiamat, the dragon monster, symbol of the primeval ocean lashing itself to fury.

The question accordingly resolves itself into this: Whether in ages long past, when the story of the composite monster Tiamat and the account of the tempter-serpent lay side by side, there was any thought that these agents of evil were one and the same being participating in different events, or, if not that, whether the beast of

[1] The most surprising variation is the occasional representation, in sculpture, of the dragon as a male, contrary to the tradition (see illustration facing p. 4). Berosus and the creation tablets are positive and emphatic as to the sex of Tiamat, and the name itself is a distinctly feminine formation.

the one narrative suggested the imagery of the other. As already said, this is improbable. The significance of the she-monster is perfectly clear. Her name told every Semitic Babylonian that she was not a reality, but a personification, a symbol of the sea. The story itself turned on the thought of the engulfing and merciless ocean conspiring with the huge fantastic masses of scurrying fog and cloud to overwhelm the world and reduce the ordered universe to primeval watery chaos, but defeated by the rays of the unconquerable sun. To set forth these things, the figure of the composite dragon came unsought; itself a creature of the imagination, a beast unseen on earth and dimly defined to the mind, but monstrous in form, enormous in bulk, and terrible in aspect and power.

With this being the serpent of the temptation has nothing in common. He is a beast of the field and licks the dust. The tradition in which he is an actor embodies a moral, and not, like the dragon-myth, a physical idea. If the seducing serpent is a historical fact, its presence in the tradition is due to its participation in the event; if, on the other hand, the narrative of the temptation be regarded as a parable and the serpent as a personification—a theory which is unproven—there is still no substantial ground for believing that the tempter-serpent either suggested the image of the dragon or, vice versa, was itself suggested by the story of that mythical monster. The snake is a natural symbol of sin. It comes spontaneously to the mind; for sin, like the serpent, is a monster of hideous mien which creeps in by stealth and infuses poison by its bite.[1] Considered in

---

[1] The serpent appears as aptly in a parable of the temptation as does the like reptile in the poem of the seven evil spirits, which has been already quoted :

> " Lock and gate do not exclude them,
> In at the door like a snake they go,
> In at the threshold like the wind they blow."

this light, the only light which can at present guide investigation, "some original connection" between the tempter-serpent and the dragon Tiamat, even so slight as borrowed imagery, is a gratuitous assumption.

A point of contact with the tradition of the temptation has been suggested as possibly found in the legend of Izdubar. "Tsitnapishtim, who dwells in 'Paradise' (on the 'island of the blessed') and in whose possession is a plant with the name 'Aged a man becomes young,' gives of this plant to Izdubar. On the way thence to Erech, it is taken from him by a snake (?). Has this plant of life," asks Jensen, from whom also the foregoing sentences are quoted, "nothing to do with the tree of life in the garden of Eden, and the snake (?), nothing to do with the hostile serpent?" (Kosmologie, S. 227). The caution which puts the suggestion in the form of a question rather than of a declaration is well observed. A connection between the garden of Eden with its tree of life and the youth-renewing plant of the island where the Babylonian Noah dwells in the enjoyment of immortality is not at all improbable. There is also no reasonable doubt as to the word snake, for the reading of the cuneiform character which represents it is now regarded as certain by both Delitzsch and Haupt, the two collators of the text. But the story of the loss of the life herb by a descendant of Noah cannot be regarded, and doubtless is not regarded by Jensen, as a parallel to the tradition of the temptation. Izdubar was journeying homeward with a plant in his hand which had rejuvenating virtue. On the way he espied a well and stopped to refresh himself. A serpent came forth, something happened to the marvellous plant,[1] a demon in the form of a lion ascended from the earth, seized the herb and disappeared. Filled with dismay Izdubar exclaimed:

[1] Jeremias renders: "The plant slipped from me" (Izdubar-Nimrod, S. 40).

"I have wrought no benefit to myself, the good has accrued to the lion of the ground." Now, did the serpent of the temptation suggest this snake detail of the story of Izdubar? There is no reason to think so; for, though the theory would be acceptable and would in nowise disparage the Hebrew account, it finds scant support in the tale, the snake playing so insignificant a part. The snake had less to do with Izdubar's loss of the plant than the lion of the ground had and is less conspicuous in the narrative.

It remains to exhibit the Hebrew doctrine of the seducing serpent. The temptation to sin came from without. The tempter-serpent is a real serpent, for it is compared with the beasts of the field, a comparison which would be pointless if the serpent described were not one of them; it possessed a natural characteristic of serpents, namely, subtilty; and the curse pronounced upon it rests upon the serpent as an animal.

The serpent tempted in his subtilty. The docility of the serpent and its tamableness were early discerned, its wisdom was proverbial (Matt. x. 16), its wiliness and spitefulness were matters of general belief. Before the domestication of the horse and the dog, while the beasts remained in their natural state, the serpent ranked high among animals for apparent intelligence and skill in securing prey.

The serpent of the temptation possessed the natural attribute of subtilty in an extraordinary and supernatural degree. The language employed is like that used in reference to Samson: "his" strength is spoken of, and the strength of that man of might was the natural attribute of man possessed in an extraordinary degree through the working of God's spirit (Judg. xvi. 5, 9, 17, with 20 and 28). Eve saw a snake, and it is not necessary to suppose that she opined more; but back of the serpent was an evil spirit (cp. the swine, Mk. v. 13). This was current interpretation in Israel, when insight into religious truth was clear. The writer of the Wisdom of Solomon says that death came into the world through the envy of the devil (ii. 23). Christ seems to have the same thought in mind when he says : "The devil was a murderer from the beginning : when he speaketh a lie, he speaketh of his own, for he is a liar and the father thereof" (John viii. 44). Paul who speaks of the serpent beguiling Eve in his craftiness, elsewhere, in evident reference to the curse upon the serpent, alludes to God bruising Satan under our feet (2 Cor. xi. 3 ; Rom. xvi. 20). John, elucidating the imagery of his visions, explains that the dragon which he sees in a certain connection is a type of "the old serpent, him that is called the devil and Satan, the deceiver of the whole world" (Rev. xii. 9).

The serpent of the temptation addressed the woman. Yet according to the narrative the animals of Paradise were unable to talk. Man differed from them in possessing the power of speech. He gave names to the beasts about him, for they as speechless creatures were unable to do this for themselves (Keil). The serpent addressed the woman in words produced by the power of Satan (cp. the demoniacs and Num. vii. 89).

As punishment for its participation in the sin, the serpent-tempter is condemned to go on its belly, eat dust, and to engage henceforth in mortal struggle with mankind. The words of the curse do not necessarily mean that the serpent had walked before it seduced man. It is remarkable that neither in the judicial sentence nor in the earlier reference to the serpent in verse 1, is anything said about its mode of locomotion (Dillmann). It may always have crept; the punishment being that henceforward its creeping and its eating or licking dust (Mic. vii. 17 ; Is. xlix. 23) shall be a symbol of degradation and a memorial of its part in man's first disobedience.

Though an irresponsible brute beast, the serpent was included in the curse. According to the Mosaic law a beast, which was made the hapless victim of man's unlawful lust, is condemned to death (Lev. xx. 15 seq.). So the serpent, although not itself accountable, was put under the curse because it had been used as an instrument of sin. But the scope of the curse is wider; the sentence addressed to the serpent terminates, not on the bodily form, but on the indwelling, intelligent spirit. The body of the serpent was but the tool, the inhabiting spirit was the guilty agent.

VIII

THE CHERUBIM

THE identity of the cherubim with the winged man-headed bulls of Assyrian and Babylonian sculpture was mooted as soon as excavation brought to light these colossal stone steers (see *e.g.* Kitto, Cyclopædia, cut 232 ; Layard, Discoveries among the Ruins of Nineveh and Babylon, p. 549 ; Studien u. Krit., 1871, S. 403). The theory received impulse from the reported discovery of the word *kirubu* in a magical text where in corresponding inscriptions *shedu*, or some other name of the winged human-headed steers, is used. Schrader states that Lenormant wrote to him in the year 1873 of the existence of a Babylonian amulet in the possession of M. de Clercq, on which *ki-ru-bu* is found in the place occupied by *shedu* in similar legends ; and Schrader adds that " this information, if confirmed, would prove the Babylonian origin of the cherubim and their identity with the colossal winged bulls which guard the entrance to temple and palace, or at least with the divine beings which these colossal figures represent (KAT²., S. 39 f.).

At a later date Lenormant himself spoke definitely in print. " It is certain," he says, "that the winged bull with a human head was called *kirubu*. The talismanic monument belonging to the collection of M. Louis de Clercq employs the term kirub (written phonetically *ki-ru-bu*) where *shedu* or the corresponding idiographic group is found elsewhere " (Les origines de l'histoire, p. 118, Eng. tr., p. 126). In the same connection, the French

SEAL WITH THE ENGRAVING

which Lenormant has compared with Ezekiel's
vision of cherubim bearing the throne
of Jehovah.

WINGED HUMAN-HEADED BULLS

stationed at a gateway of Sargon's palace. The arch that once spanned the
passage sprang from the heads of the larger bulls. Height of
larger bulls, eighteen feet.

savant drew attention to the scene engraved on a cylinder seal, in which he saw the counterpart of the imagery of Ezekiel's vision. The prophet beheld "four living creatures" or cherubim which, in Lenormant's opinion, were arranged two and two, back to back, and went "each one straight forward" toward the four quarters. Over their heads and borne by them was a crystal pavement; and above the pavement the likeness of a throne, as the appearance of a sapphire stone, and upon the throne the likeness as of a man enveloped in shining light. It was the appearance of the likeness of the glory of God. On the cylinder seal referred to is depicted a marvellous boat terminating at each end in a human half-figure. On the boat two winged bulls, each with the face of a man, stand back to back. Their position necessarily presupposes two other like animals hidden by them, which support the other side of the pavement that they bear on their shoulders. On this pavement is a throne; upon which a bearded god is seated, clad in a long robe, with a tiara on his head and a short sceptre and a ring in his hand. By his side stands a personage of inferior size as though awaiting his commands; like the man in the vision of the tenth chapter of Ezekiel, the man clothed in linen with the writer's ink-horn by his side who receives the commands of Jehovah.

Friedrich Delitzsch has also adopted the theory of the identity of the cherubim with the colossal winged bulls of Babylonia. The argument as recast by him is, 1. The living beings with wings of bird and face of man which Ezekiel describes [1] bear a remarkable external resemblance to the winged human-headed bulls of Babylonia. 2. The function of the colossal steers of Babylonia is also the same as that of the cherubim of the Hebrews: they stand as watchers at the entrance of temples and

---

[1] They have, however, the face of eagle, ox, and lion as well as that of man.

palaces, guarding the precincts from intrusion; and they appear—as *e.g.* on the boat engraved on the cylinder—like the cherubim in Ezekiel's vision, as bearers of the throne of God.[1] 3. The strongest evidence exists, however, in the interchangeability of the names *kirubu* and *shedu*, as is proven by the inscription in the possession of M. Louis de Clercq (Paradies, S. 150–153).

Twenty years have elapsed since the letter of Lenormant was written to Schrader. The talismanic monument has not been produced in public, it would seem, and its reading remains unconfirmed. The cautiousness observed by Schrader in basing an argument on it is commended by a recent writer who signs himself v. F. (ZA., vol. i., 68–70). "None other of the Assyriologists," he says further, "who know the collection of M. de Clercq, has confirmed the news;" and he concludes his note on the subject with the remark that, "so long as nothing authentic is known in regard to the amulet which is at present in the possession of M. de Clercq, we must acknowledge that proof has not been furnished of the employment of the word *kirubu* to designate the Assyrian bull divinities."

Boscawen seeks to identify the scorpion men, *aqrabu-amêlu*, who guarded the way which Izdubar was obliged to pass, with the cherubim of Genesis (B. and O. Record, vol. iii., 145 seq.). The duties which devolved upon the aqrabu-men and the cherubim are somewhat similar, but the names are not akin. *Aqrabu*, עקרב, etc., have no etymological connection with כרוב.

---

[1] Delitzsch holds also that the seven demons of Babylonian mythology are " in last analysis identical with the bull divinities" and " are repeatedly called

So much as to the efforts made to find the counterpart of the Hebrew cherubim in Babylonian thought and art. But what were they in themselves? What was their nature? Cheyne sees in the cherub "a form of speech retained from myth-making times, and meaning the storm-cloud or (as Professor Tiele suggests) the cloud masses which seem to guard the portals of the sky, and on which the sun god appears to issue forth at break of day" (Prophecies of Isaiah, vol. i., p. 115, ii., 298). Now if cherub is a common noun and means storm-cloud—a natural object to which Semitic nature worshippers would, of course, at once ascribe a spirit—the imagery of the psalmist is satisfied when he says: "Thick darkness was under his feet and he rode upon a cherub and did fly; yea, he flew swiftly upon the wings of the wind" (Ps. xviii. 9-10). If it means storm-cloud, much that is predicated of the cherubim is also met; for the storm-cloud moves through space, could bear the visible glory of Jehovah, betoken his indignation, and warn against intruding into his presence. If cherubim signify storm-clouds, they could also be stationed at the entrance of the garden with the flaming lightning to keep the way to the tree of life. It is impossible, however, that the storm-cloud as a thing animated and revered as divine by heathen polytheists is intended in the Hebrew scriptures; and it is difficult to reconcile the interpretation of the word cherub as a common noun meaning merely the storm-cloud with the biblical descriptions in which

the 'throne-bearers of the gods,' thus resembling the Merkaba [or cherubim] of Ezekiel" (Paradies, S. 152). But this resemblance vanishes if, as Jensen argues, the word *guzalû*, translated "throne-bearer," means rather "a commissioner" (Kosmologie, S. 390). And there is no proof that the seven demons are "in last analysis identical with the bull divinities." They are indeed like the bulls called *shedu*; but this means that the seven demons and the bulls belong to the category of inferior supernatural beings, for as is well known *shedu* is a general designation for demon, whether good or evil. It is the Hebrew word שֵׁד.

cherubim are represented, emblematically it is true,
yet distinctly, as intelligent beings with strength like
the ox, courage like the lion, flight like the eagle;
celestial beings, it would seem, with special office, commissioned to bear Jehovah's glory, indicate his nearness,
and guard his presence from intrusion. Now Franz
Delitzsch believed with Cheyne that "in Ezekiel as in
other parts of the Bible we trace the connection between
the cherubim and the thunder-storm, in which God
manifests himself. There is the same fire of lightning
running to and fro, and the same roar as of rumbling
wheels." And he held the cherub to be "a creation of
Semitic heathenism which deified the powers of nature"
(Schaff-Herzog, Art. Cherubim; Delitzsch, Genesis[5], S.
114). But he was not blind to the fact that the biblical
writers represent the cherubim as animate beings. How
then does he reconcile the two conceptions? He thinks
that after the storm-cloud had been deified by the heathen,
it was denied deity by the Hebrews, but left animate.
It was not a storm-cloud lowering in the sky, it was not
a mere power of nature, and it was not a god; yet it was
animate. "The religion of revelation depotentiated the
cherubs as it did other heathen deifications of natural
forces, making of them powers ($\delta\upsilon\nu\acute{\alpha}\mu\epsilon\iota\varsigma$) subordinated
to the Lord of hosts ($\kappa\acute{\upsilon}\rho\iota\sigma\varsigma$ $\tau\tilde{\omega}\nu$ $\delta\upsilon\nu\acute{\alpha}\mu\epsilon\omega\nu$). It proceeded
on the conception that there is a heaven where God is
surrounded by superhuman beings, among whom are
those who belong in the immediate presence of him who
sits on the throne, are his bearers when he is manifesting
himself in his glory in the world, and are the guardians
of the place of his presence, warding off everything unlike in character and unprivileged to approach."

This is the explanation offered by the devout Franz
Delitzsch. The facts are perhaps not all in, upon which
the final solution of the question depends; but in the

meanwhile it must be confessed that Delitzsch has
erected a stupendous theory on scanty evidence. When
the testimony that is offered is sifted, the interpretation of
cherub as storm-cloud seems to rest, first, upon the passage in the Psalms where it is said of Jehovah that
" thick darkness was under his feet and he rode upon a
cherub and did fly ; yea, he flew swiftly upon the wings
of the wind :" and secondly, upon the possibility of discerning the lightning in " the flame of a sword which
turned every way, to keep the way of the tree of life."
In the great body of passages, however, which relate to
the cherubim a reference to the storm-cloud is, to say the
least, not manifest. Moreover, the evident difficulty
which Delitzsch experiences in reconciling the prepon-
derating or, quite possibly, constant biblical description of
the cherubim as intelligent beings with the interpretation
of the word cherub as storm-cloud is against such interpretation. A minor feature of the delineation is forced to
outbalance the major feature. Likewise, no conclusive
evidence has yet been furnished that the winged, human-
headed bulls of Babylonia symbolized the storm-cloud.
This explanation of the bull divinities also seems to rest
ultimately upon the passage quoted from the Hebrew
psalm, the idea deduced from the words of the Hebrew
poet being imposed upon the Babylonian bulls. Indeed
the Babylonians represented the storm-cloud as a bird,
the well-known Zu bird ; while the winged, human-
headed bulls seem, like the Hebrew cherubim, to typify
beings with the strength of an ox, the free motion of a
bird, and the intelligence of a man.[1]

Whatever may have been denoted by the cherubim and

[1] No evidence has been adduced to prove that " the bull begotten of the god
Zu " (IV R. 23 ; cited by Cheyne, Isaiah, vol. ii. 296) has any reference to the
winged, human-headed bulls. Professor Sayce thinks that the colossal bulls
which guarded the entrance to temple and palace " represented divine beings,
the gods or genii of the household " (Hibbert Lectures, 1887, p. 290).

whatever be the outcome of the search after analogues among other peoples, it is important to emphasize the fact that the delineations of them in art and their forms as seen in vision were, like modern pictures of angels, symbols only. The representation in wood, stone, or embroidered cloth, and the evanescent appearance which flitted before the mind of seer, awakening a sense of the dread presence of God and quickening expectancy of a manifestation of his glory, were not regarded as the thing itself. They were not always the same in form, for they resulted from the struggle to approximate the truth ; they were felt to fall below the conception ; they were known to be merely the image which betokened the greater reality. In the account of the garden of Eden, the writer is not speaking of images placed at the portal, but of the reality itself, stationed to keep the way.

IX

CAIN AND ABEL

THE search which has been prosecuted in Babylonian literature for counterparts to the Hebrew records has not been neglected in the case of the narrative of Cain and Abel. Professor Sayce has thrown out suggestions in his Hibbert Lectures which tend to identify the god Tammuz with Abel.[1] His argument is best presented by copious quotation. "Tammuz," he says, "must have been the primitive Sun-god of Eridu. . . . It is even possible that the boar whose tusk proved fatal to Adonis [the Greek Tammuz] may originally have been Adar [the Sun-god of Nipur (p. 153)] himself. Adar . . . was called the 'lord of the swine' in the Accadian period, and the Semitic abhorrence of the animal may have used it to symbolize the ancient rivalry between the Sun-god of Nipur and the Sun-god of Eridu. Those who would see in the Cain and Abel of Scripture the representatives of elemental deities and who follow Dr. Oppert in explaining the name of Abel by the Babylonian *ablu*, 'the son,' slightly transformed by a popular etymol-

[1] For other suggestions—some based on mistranslations, due of course not to lack of scholarship on the part of the translator, but to the unadvanced stage of the science—all dubious and speculative and making no claim of furnishing a document parallel to the Hebrew tradition, see Lenormant, Les origines de l'histoire, chap. iv

ogy, may be inclined to make them the Adar and Tammuz of Chaldean faith." The name Tammuz means in "the original Accadian 'the son of life' . . . interpreted by the Semites as meaning 'the offspring.'" [1] "As Abel in the Old Testament is 'a keeper of sheep,' so, too, Tammuz in Babylonia was accounted a shepherd." "The title 'lord of the pig' connects Adar with the Arês of Greek mythology, who in the form of the wild boar slew the Sun-god Tammuz; while the title [also applied to him] 'lord of the date'—the chief fruit of Babylonia—reminds us of Cain, who was 'a tiller of the ground'" (Hibbert Lectures, pp. 236, 232, 245, and 153, note 6; and cp. p. 186).

The combination of facts and fancies presented in these extracts is ingenious, but the particulars have no evidential value.

1. Tammuz indeed probably means "son of life" and Abel may be a modification of the Assyrian word *aplu*, son. But these facts are far from establishing the identity of the two. The name in each case has its occasion and its appropriateness. The god who, though dying annually, returns to life with each recurring year, is beautifully and aptly named "son of life." The bare and bald word son likewise might be fittingly bestowed on the child Abel, corresponding to the appellatives Adam *human being*, Eve *life*, Cain *formation;* but it would not be more appropriate than the designation *breath, vanity,* the posthumous name given to him which told the story of his untimely end, and the name by which in fact he was remembered.

2. Abel was a keeper of sheep; and Tammuz, it is true, was likewise called a shepherd. The passage cited

[1] Not, however, as meaning "the only son," as might be gathered from Professor Sayce's additional statement; at least not so interpreted in the passage cited in proof, II R. 36, 54.

in proof forms the introduction to a brief text (IV R. 27, No. 1), of which the first two lines are as follows :

" Shepherd, lord, god Tammuz, husband of goddess Ishtar,
King of the nether world, king of the [watery] abode, shepherd."

But the title given to the god is not distinctive. It does not belong exclusively to Tammuz. The god Gir, son of Shamash, whom Professor Sayce will scarcely identify with Tammuz after what he has said on p. 233, is also called a shepherd (ASKT., p. 105, 10). Nor does the title describe Tammuz as a keeper of sheep. It is figurative. It was in constant use as a synonym for ruler. As Professor Sayce himself says (p. 245): "The Chaldeans were a people of agriculturists and herdsmen ; their monarchs were addressed as shepherds." The fact that Tammuz is called a shepherd affords, therefore, no proof of any intention to describe him as a keeper of sheep or even as patron of a guild. He is hailed as ruler.[1]

3. Whether Tammuz be regarded as symbolical of the sun dying in winter and reviving with the return of spring, or as the sun-god of spring whose foe was the summer heat (Sayce, Hibbert Lectures, p. 231), or as the vegetation of spring destroyed by the scorching rays of the eastern sun (Jensen, Kosmologie, S. 480), the essential idea in the nature-myth was the annual return of Tammuz to life. The revival of the dead god is the pith of the tale. But Abel whom Cain slew rose not again : his life on earth was extinguished ; as a link in the

[1] In another passage in which Professor Sayce, assuming an error to have been committed by the writer of the tablet, sees a reference to " some deity, probably Tammuz, who is called 'the divine son' in the Accadian text" (Hibbert Lectures, p. 489), and who is presently termed shepherd, it is the translator and not the Assyrian scribe who is at fault There is no allusion to Tammuz. The word which is looked upon with suspicion, forms part of the royal name Ashurbanipal, and the paragraph is a prayer in behalf of that monarch. King Ashurbanipal is the shepherd.

genealogical chain he dropped out, the godly line of
Adam descended through another.

The Hebrew narrative stands accordingly as yet alone.
The Hebrew scriptures furnish the only document known
in which the tradition has been transmitted and can be
studied. The preservation of the tradition by the religious teachers of Israel was due to its ethical value. It
exhibits the conduct that is acceptable to God and traces
the downward progress of sin.

The two brothers on reaching man's estate devoted
themselves the one to agriculture, the other to the tending of flocks. In process of time each brought an offering unto the Lord. The offerings were alike in being
valuable gifts, the product of the offerer's daily toil, presented unto the same God; yet "the Lord had respect
unto Abel and to his offering, but unto Cain and to his
offering he had not respect." God looked on the character of the man (as is evident from v. 7). Abel was accepted because his heart was right towards God: he was
righteous (Mat. xxiii. 35; 1 John iii. 12); he believed at
least that God is, and that God is the rewarder of them
that diligently seek him, and he conformed his conduct
to this belief. Cain, on the other hand, was a wicked
man, and his character was speedily revealed to the
world. Instead of being incited to earnest searching of
heart because his offering was rejected, he allowed anger
to fill his soul, refused the exhortation to strive against
sin, committed murder, and became hardened, denying
knowledge of his brother's whereabouts and disclaiming
responsibility for him; and when judgment was passed
on the awful deed, he manifested no regrets for the sin
but only concern about the punishment. Such a fearful
advance had man made in the career of wickedness.

God had accepted Abel and his offering, and had rejected Cain. At the dawn of history the cardinal truth

was made known to man that " the sacrifice of the wicked is an abomination to the Lord, but the prayer of the upright is his delight" (Prov. xv. 8).[1]

[1] In this narrative the writer tacitly assumes that man was increasing on the earth. Cain foreboded danger at the hands of his kindred as soon as his foul deed should become known to them. Relationships were constantly becoming more remote. There were people more closely bound by blood and interest and affection to the one brother than to the other, and Cain expressed the fear that the impulse to take vengeance would be followed. The increase of man on earth is involved in Cain's marriage also. He had a wife; his sister perhaps or his half-sister or his niece. In early ages no impropriety existed or was felt in such marriages. Abraham had a half-sister to wife, and Nahor a niece (Gen. xx. 12; xi. 27, 29); and Egyptian princes not infrequently married their sisters.

X

CAINITES AND SETHITES.

SANCHONIATHON, the "philosopher of Tyre," has given the Phœnician account of the origin and development of human civilization. This description of man's progress presents points of contact, and is frequently compared, with the genealogy and work of the Cainites as recorded in the fourth chapter of Genesis. The Phœnician historian, as reported by Eusebius from Philo of Byblos, wrote as follows:

"Of the wind Kolpia and his wife Baau, which is interpreted 'night,' were born Aion and Protogonos, mortal men thus named; and Aion discovered how to nourish oneself from trees. Their offspring were called Genos and Genea. They dwelt in Phœnicia. When droughts occurred, they lifted their hands to the heavens towards the sun (for they thought that it was the only lord of heaven) calling it Beelsamin, which in Phœnician means 'lord of heaven.'

Of the race [or, according to the Latin version, of Genos the son] of Aion and Protogonos were again begotten mortal children, whose names were Phos, Pur, and Phlox. These found out the method of generating fire by rubbing together pieces of wood, and taught its use. They begat sons who surpassed them in size and excellence, and whose names were given to the mountains of which they were the lords; thus Mount Cassius [in Syria] and Lebanon and Antilebanon and Brathu took their names from them.

Of these was begotten [Sa]memroumos or Hupsouranios. He dwelt in Tyre, and found out how to make huts of reeds and rushes and papyrus. He quarrelled with his brother Ousoos. The latter was the first to invent a covering for the body out of the skins of the wild beasts he was able to catch, . . . He also, having taken a tree and lopped off its boughs, was the first who dared to put out to sea. He consecrated two pillars to fire and wind; and he worshipped them and poured out to them the blood of the wild beasts he had taken. When these men were dead, their survivors consecrated staves to them and worshipped pillars and kept feasts in their honor year by year.

Long afterwards, Agreus and Halieus were born of the race of Hupsouranios. They were the originators of hunting and fishing, and from them hunters and fishermen are named. Of these were begotten two brothers, the discoverers of iron and its working. One of these, Chrusor, practised words, spells, and divinations; he invented the fishing-hook, bait and line, and the raft; and he was the first to use sails: therefore men worshipped him after his death as a god. Some say his brothers thought of making walls of bricks.

Afterwards, of his race, two youths were born, Technites and earthy Autochthon. They devised mixing stubble with the clay of bricks and drying them in the sun; and they also invented roofing. By these others were begotten, one of whom was called Agros, the other Agroueros or Agrotes. They devised the addition of courts, enclosures, and cellars to houses. From them come rustics and such as hunt with dogs, called wanderers and Titans.

From them also sprang Amunos and Magos, who taught men to construct villages and tend flocks. Of these came Misor and Suduk, that is 'active' and 'just;' and they discovered the use of salt. From Misor sprang Taautos, who invented the writing of the first letters, and whom the Egyptians called Thoth. From Suduk descended the Dioscuri or Cabiri or Corybantes or Samothracian deities. They were the first to invent a ship. From these descended others who discovered medicinal herbs and the cure of poisons, and spells."

A number of Semitic words occur in this passage. Baau and Beelsamen, Samemrounos, Misor and Suduk are at once recognized. But the names are for the most part Greek, and are doubtless translations of the original Phœnician words. Proceeding on these facts Orelli, who edited an edition of Sanchoniathon in 1826, and Lenormant would retranslate Aion, "lifetime," into its Semitic homophone and partial synonym *chavvah*, "life," *i.e.* Eve; Protogonos, "first-born," they would render by Adam, "man;" while in Genos they see the Grecized form of Cain. Thus at once the close relationship between the story as told by Sanchoniathon and the tradition which was current in Israel becomes apparent: for according to Sanchoniathon's account, when translated back into the original Semitic, the first mortals were Adam the first and Eve, who discovered the art of nourishing oneself from the fruit of trees; of this couple were born Cain and Caina, and from Cain proceeded a race which became noted for its contributions to the arts and for its introduction of new occupations among men. But in spite of these striking results, the attempt of Orelli and Lenormant is a failure. Philologically it is wild, and at the same time it appears to be based on a misconception of the Phœnician story. The most that sober scholarship can say has been said by Dillmann in his remark that the closest resemblance of the Cainite narrative with the Phœnician legend lies in the connecting of the stages of civilization with certain names, and that it is especially worthy of comparison that "two brothers appear as the discoverers of iron and its working, and one of them practised words, spells, and divination, with which compare the double sense of *charash* in Hebrew and Aramaic" (Genesis,⁶ S. 102).

Persons are not intended by the Phœnician narrator. In his story the proper names are common nouns. This was clear to his fellow-countrymen, and was not obscured in the early Greek and Latin translations. Two mortals, Sanchoniathon says, were brought into existence, Duration-of-life and First-born; of whom the former discovered the nourishment that is in the fruit of trees. From this couple proceeded Race or Family and Stock, and from Race were born three mortals, Light,

Fire, and Flame, who discovered how to produce fire by friction. From these came stalwart beings who were lords of the mountains. Of them in turn sprang two brothers, named respectively One-from-high-heaven and Ousoos [a name of which the meaning is unknown]. The brothers were hostile. The one invented huts of reeds and dwelt at Tyre : the other was a hunter in a primitive sort of way, who caught animals as best he could, used their skin for clothing and their blood for libations ; who, discerning that logs float, essayed into the sea on a tree-trunk, and who worshipped the elements. Long afterwards, of the race of the hut-dweller, Hunter and Fisher were born, who introduced hunting and fishing. Then came the two who discovered iron and its working, of whom one Chrusor [the meaning of which name is unknown] introduced fishing implements, devised the raft, employed sails, and used incantations. Afterwards, in his line, appeared Artificer and Earthy-Native, who made bricks of clay and introduced the roofing of houses [commonly with earth]. Of these were born Field and Rustic, with whom began husbandry, the addition of courts, enclosures, and cellars to houses, and hunting with dogs. From them sprang Ammos [perhaps meaning " defence "] and Magos [meaning unknown], who introduced villages and the tending of flocks. From these came Rectitude and Justice, who found out the use of salt [and who regulated civil life (Dillmann)]. Of Rectitude was born Taautos, the Egyptian Thoth, who introduced the use of letters in writing ; while from Justice sprang the Dioscuri [the protectors of ships in storms]. From these sprang the discoverers of medicinal herbs.

Sanchoniathon rehearses his tale in the form of a genealogy ; but it is probable that he never intended it as an actual family history. The links consist of abstract conceptions, occupations, and natural objects connected with modes of life, the names undisguised. The nouns mirror the new and salient feature of the age under review. The story is a sagacious and remarkably successful attempt to exhibit the characteristics of the successive stages of human development, beginning in primitive times and extending to the date when the description was penned. The author describes the several ages by indicating the novelty that marks progress. The characteristics were:

Of the 1st age. Birth of man and mere monotonous duration of life. Food consisted of fruits.

Of the 2d age. Lineage or family.

Of the 3d age. Fire, as produced and employed by man.

Of the 4th age. The mountain chieftains.

Of the 5th age. Settled life over against roving life. Huts of reeds; and clothing of skin, floating on logs, worship of the elements.

Of the 6th age. The hunter and the fisher.

Of the 7th age. The ironworkers; fishing implements, raft of logs, use of sails, incantation.

Of the 8th age. The artificer and the native one, of earth, who make bricks of clay and roof houses.

Of the 9th age. The field and the rustic; exhibited in husbandry, enlargement of houses [for storing produce], employment of dogs in hunting.

Of the 10th age. Towns built and flocks tended.

Of the 11th age. Rectitude and justice; seen in the regulation of civil life. Salt used.

Of the 12th age. Alphabet introduced, the complete ship.

Of the 13th age. Medicine.

The scheme is admirably worked out. The floating log is gradually developed into the complete ship, the hut of reeds into the spacious, roofed house of bricks, the rude seizure of animals into hunting with dogs.[1]

When the Phœnician narrative is scanned, it loses greatly in resemblance to the Hebrew account. But independently of this interpretation of the Phœnician story, the theory of its connection, however remote, with the Hebrew tradition is unnecessary and for the following reasons improbable : 1. Though the Phœnician tale be pure speculation, yet since it treats of a theme which is incidentally mentioned in the Hebrew account of the Cainites, it must show points of resemblance to the Hebrew record. Certain facts in the history of human progress are evident to the thinking man and must find place in every thoughtful narrative of man's advance in civilization. These discernible facts form points of resemblance, even though the several narratives in which they occur are independent of each other in origin. 2. The Phœnician story is local in its details : Phœnicia is the abode of men when they are still naked and without fire ; the race begins its development under the shadow of Lebanon and Antilebanon and Cassius ; in the neighborhood of Tyre the first hut-builder dwells ; the metal discovered and worked is iron, a product of the Syrian mountains ; the sea allures the venturesome, provokes the mind to invention, and opens a highway to the papyrus of the neighboring Nile. The scene of the Hebrew narrative is the far east ; the first man dwelt in Eden, near the Tigris and Euphrates rivers, and Cain journeyed into the land of Nod on the east of Eden. 3. The names in the Phœnician story are common nouns, and denote abstract ideas, or trades and occu-

---

[1] The biblical picture is less detailed. 1. Man ; his food the fruit of trees, and God the object of worship. 2. Sin. 3. Clothing of skin. 4. Tilling soil and tending flocks. 5. The community or town. 6. Nomad shepherds with movable tents, musical instruments, copper and iron working.

pations, or natural objects connected with modes of life. In the Hebrew narrative the names do not mark advancing civilization nor even denote trades, unless in the case of the sons of Lamech; and the list contains two examples of the compound proper names in vogue among the Semites, Mehujael and Methushael, of which the latter has a decided Babylonian cast. 4. The Phœnician tale is told in the manner of oriental philosophy, putting its speculations or its knowledge of the development of civilization figuratively in the form of a genealogy and treating the novel feature of each age as a person and a progenitor because embodied in and transmitted by successive generations of the human race. The Hebrew narrative, on the other hand, has the characteristics of human family history, concrete, personal, living.

A common element, indeed, these two accounts have. Each is based on the belief that man came forth from the hands of the Creator with capacity, but without attainment. He was ushered naked into the world and for a time he lived in it naked, without knowledge of the resources of inanimate nature and without apprehension of the utility of animals; but created with powers of discernment and ability to subdue the earth and all things in it unto himself.

A Babylonian tradition is available for comparison with the account of the Sethites or ten patriarchs which is given in the fifth chapter of Genesis. In the second book of his history, Berosus enumerates the ten kings

of the Chaldeans who reigned before the deluge.[1] He
says [2] that

"The first king was Alorus of [the city of [5]] Babylon, a Chaldean. [He gave out a report about himself that God had appointed him to be shepherd of the people.[3]] He reigned ten
sars. [A sar is thirty-six hundred years.[3]]

And afterwards Alaparus [his son [5] reigned three sars[3] [5]].

And [after him [3]] Amelon [a Chaldean [6]], who was of [the city
of [3] [5]] Pantibiblon [reigned thirteen sars[3]].

Then Ammenon the Chaldean [of Pantibiblon reigned twelve
sars[3] [5]].

Then Megalarus of the city of Pantibiblon, and he reigned
eighteen sars.

And after him Daonus the shepherd of Pantibiblon reigned ten
sars.

Then Euedorachus of Pantibiblon reigned eighteen sars.

Then Amempsinus, a Chaldean of Laranchae, reigned; and he,
the eighth, was king ten sars.

Next Otiartes, a Chaldean of Laranchae, reigned; and he [the
ninth [1]] was king eight sars.

And [last of all [3]], upon the death of Otiartes, his son Xisuthrus
reigned eighteen sars. In his time the great deluge occurred.

Thus, when summed up, the kings are ten; and the sars are
one hundred and twenty [or four hundred and thirty-two thousand
years, reaching to the flood [1]]."

This catalogue resembles the Sethite genealogy recorded in the fifth chapter of Genesis in that it is restricted to antediluvians, contains the names of ten persons, and terminates with the hero of the flood. The
difference between the lists, at least as they now lie before us, is however as marked as the agreement. The
corresponding names in the two catalogues bear no out-

[1] Syncellus quoting Alexander Polyhistor.
[2] Syncellus quoting Apollodorus.
[3] Syncellus quoting Abydenus.
[4] Syncellus quoting Abydenus concerning the deluge.
[5] Eusebius, Armenian Chronicle, quoting Alexander Polyhistor.
[6] Eusebius, Armenian Chronicle, quoting Abydenus.

ward resemblance to each other[1] and the years ascribed
to the corresponding names stand in no arithmetic ratio
to each other; the Hebrew register is silent as to the
rank or title of the men whose genealogy it records, while
the Babylonian enumerates kings; the one is a lineage in
which each member is related by blood to both his pred-
ecessor and successor, the other is a line of kings of
whom the father is not always followed by the son, but a
new dynasty occasionally arises; the one gives a genealogy of the human race from its origin, the other begins
with the first king of Babylon. But all these differences
may perhaps lie on the surface. 1. The Babylonian list,
as it now exists, contains indeed the names of kings only,
but this may be an error which grew out of the felt need

[1] Internal resemblance may, of course, exist notwithstanding external unlikeness. Before, however, the meaning of the names in the two lists can be
successfully compared, the original Babylonian form of those which Berosus
gives must be determined. And this is difficult. But the difficulty is not due
to contradictions in our present manuscripts. The names have been transmitted by them with substantial unanimity, except in the case of the third,
fifth, seventh, and ninth. The references are to the footnote on the preceding
page.

1. Ἄλωρος.[2,3]	Alorus.[5,6]
2. Ἀλάπαρος.[2,3]	Alaparus.[5,6]
3. Ἀμήλων.[2] Ἀμίλλαρος.[3]	Almelon.[5,6]
4. Ἀμμένων.[2,3]	Ammenon.[5,6]
5. Μεγάλαρος.[2,3]	Amegalarus.[5,6]
6. Δάωνος.[2] Δαώς.[3]	Davonus.[5,6]
7. Εὐεδώραχος.[2] Εὐεδώρεσχος.[3]	Edoranchus.[5] Edoreschus.[6]
8. Ἀμεμψινός.[2]	Amemphsinus.[6]
9. Ἀρδάτης.[1] Ὠτιάρτης.[2]	Otiartes.[6]
10. Ξίσουθρος.[1,2] Σίσουθρος.[3] Σίσιθρος.[4]	Xisuthrus.[5,6]

Variations of minor importance, frequently alluded to, are Ἀλάσπαρος and
Ἀμφίς (Syncel., p. 18 A, a passage full of errors) as second and eighth kings;
Μεγάλανος (Cod. Paris., 1711) as fifth; Amen phsinus as the eighth, occurring
in both places where the name is found in the text, but corrected in the mar-
gin to Amemphsinus; and Scaliger's readings Ἀεδώρεσχος' and often Σείσουθρος.

Of the many attempts made to discover the original Babylonian form of
these names and to identify them with the corresponding ones in the Hebrew
list, that of Delitzsch, meagre as its results are, has not been superseded
(Paradies, S. 149). Perhaps the latest essay in this line is Hommel's (PSBA,
xv., 243 seq.).

to bestow some title on these men commensurate with
their renown. If not kings, they were famous. The cuneiform tablets which contain an account of the deluge are
at least three hundred years earlier than Berosus, and do
not describe Xisuthrus as king; nor does the biblical account so describe Noah. 2. In the Babylonian list the
descent of the government from father to son is asserted
in two instances only, namely, from the first king to the
second and from the ninth to the tenth; and the existence of three successive dynasties, namely of Babylon,
of Pantibiblon, and of Laranchae, seems to be affirmed.
But the Hebrew asserts kinship, however remote, between
the successive links. Still the genealogy which is recorded by the Hebrew writer is not unlikely just such a
one as might be constructed out of the line of English
monarchs who have reigned since the Norman conquest,
by the selection of ten names in their chronological sequence which would represent the different dynasties and
at the same time would exhibit the unbroken descent
from the Conqueror. 3. Each of the ten patriarchs is
assigned a prolonged life; each of the ten kings has a
greatly longer reign. The contrast is twofold; between
the number of years in corresponding cases, and between
length of life and length of reign. But instead of this
difference indicating non-identity of the two lines, it may
be found, when the Semitic tradition is fully known, to
afford a simpler explanation than that usually offered for
the duration of life which is ascribed to the patriarchs.
4. The symmetry of the numbers in the Babylonian
transmission is open to the suspicion of being artificial.
The number of kings is ten; the sum of their united
reigns is one hundred and twenty sar, a multiple of ten
and of the basal number of the Babylonian duodeci-
mal system. There are three reigns of ten sar each,
three of eighteen sar each, and three successive reigns

which taken together make ten and eighteen sar. Taking
the reigns in the order in which they occur, we have as
their duration the series 10, 18+10, 18, 10, 18, 10, 8,
and 18.

What then is the relation of these lists to each other?
It is difficult to say. The wiser course is to suspend judgment for the present and allow the question to remain
open. The facts are capable of two interpretations : either
the two catalogues are fundamentally different, having
been constructed for different purposes, yet as they deal
with prominent persons belonging to the same historic
age and to the same country, cross each other at various
points, and culminate in the same individual ; or else—and
this is the more probable theory—when the accretions
and transformations of centuries are removed, the two
catalogues will be found to represent the same tradition.

XI

THE SONS OF GOD

THE intermarriage of the sons of God with the daughters of man is related in the sixth chapter of Genesis. No parallel to this account has been discovered. Investigation is accordingly shut up to the question of the interpretation of the biblical narrative.

At least two conceptions of the phrase " sons of God " in this passage are known to have existed at the beginning of the Christian era, and a third co-existed with them in the early Christian centuries. 1. The sons of God were sons of the mighty of the earth who married with women of the lower classes. This view is represented by the Samaritan version, by the Greek translation of Symmachus, and by the targums of Onkelos and Jonathan. 2. The sons of God were angels who, leaving or having left their first estate, took wives from among the children of men. This view is represented by the Book of Enoch, by Philo and Josephus, and by the most ancient of the fathers, such as Justin Martyr, Clement of Alexandria, and Tertullian. 3. The sons of God were the Sethites. They were attracted by the beauty of women who did not belong to the godly line, married with them and became secularized. This is the view of early churchmen like Julius Africanus, Chrysostom and Cyril of Alexandria, Augustine, and Jerome.

The first interpretation has been generally abandoned as unwarranted. The second has many advocates, numbering among them the great exegetes Franz Delitzsch and August Dillmann. Dillmann takes a low view. He finds in the narrative a reminder of heathen mythology ; and he holds that the account has been drawn from ancient legends of the giants, beings half god and half man. Delitzsch, on the other hand, like Justin Martyr of old and Kurtz among modern scholars, entertains a high view of the passage. His argument is substantially as follows: 1. Everywhere else in the Old Testament the phrase "sons of God" means angels and must have the same meaning here. The name refers to the nature of angels, not to their office. The official title is *mal'ach*, messenger. They are sons of God by nature, whether they are good or evil. 2. The sons of *God* are contrasted with the daughters of *man*, the divine is contrasted with the human : for the expression "daughters of man" is to be understood in the light of v. 1, where man means mankind in general, and not that portion of the race which had become estranged from God. 3. The phrase "to take a wife" means entrance into permanent married relation. The account does not speak of single acts of intercourse, but of permanent and, so far as the angels are concerned, unnatural relation with women. It must, therefore, be assumed that the angels assumed human bodies and not that they manifested themselves transiently in human form.[1] The case is parallel to later instances of possession by evil spirits. Demons, having taken possession of the bodies of [wicked] men and using them as instruments, married the daughters of men. "In this," he adds, "we perhaps go beyond the narrator, who here reduces to the kernel of truth the obscene stories which heathen mythology delights to elaborately embellish."

In confirmation of his argument Delitzsch appeals to Jude 6 : "Angels which kept not their own principality,

---

[1] On the basis of Gen. vi. Kurtz founds the doctrine that angels are not pure spirits and incorporeal, but are possessed of bodies.

but left their proper habitation, he hath kept in everlasting bonds under darkness unto the judgment of the great day." But 1. The very point at issue is whether Jude is referring to the sixth chapter of Genesis or not.[1] The existence of fallen angels was known, even if their fall is not recorded in the sixth chapter of Genesis. Satan was a fallen being and an outcast from heaven while man was yet in Eden. His angels also, for whom together with him the eternal fire had been prepared, fell from their first estate of holiness (Matt. xxv. 41 ; Rev. xii. 9). Jude may have these events in mind. Again in Is. xxiv. 21-23, on Delitzsch's own interpretation, a punishment of angelic hosts and earthly princes is described which bears close resemblance to the passage in Jude ; and Cheyne understands that Jude and Peter and John (Rev. xx. 2-3) and the author of the Book of Enoch in another place (xviii. 13-16) refer to this passage. It is begging the question, therefore, and precarious to assert that Jude attributes the fall of angels to their intermarriage with mankind. And 2. While Delitzsch regards the narrative in Genesis as history, he fails to explain how angels by taking possession of the bodies of men could, as indwelling spirits, experience the mystery of human affection or gratify a carnal appetite. It would be the human instrument, not the indwelling controlling demon, that would feel. Kurtz is right. If angels entered into marriage relation with women, they are corporeal beings (History of the Old Covenant, i., p. 100 seq.).

The chief objections to the theory which regards the sons of God in the sixth chapter of Genesis as angels are two. 1. A very early interpretation of the passage, perhaps the most ancient known, that of the Samaritan version, explained the sons of God as human beings.

---

[1] The word " these " in v. 7 may refer either to the angels of v. 6 or to the inhabitants of Sodom.

This is strange if the title was given by the Israelites to angels exclusively. The view that angels are meant seems to be a later growth; it was, at all events, the teaching of a special school among the Jews of the first century, and not of the whole or even most influential part of the Jewish church of that day. 2. The second objection to the theory in question is that it contradicts the Scripture doctrine of angels. No biblical writer anywhere else countenances the idea that angels could or would enter into married relation with mankind. The uniform representation of Scripture elsewhere is that the passions of demons, irrespective of the form of wickedness into which they may drive the possessed, and the emotions of unfallen angels are without exception spiritual, not carnal. It is doctrine novel to Scripture that woman's beauty could arouse animal love in angel or demon.

The third theory, namely, that the sons of God were the godly race of Seth, is satisfactory. For 1. According to a very early interpretation, the most ancient one perhaps that is attested, men are meant. 2. Judged from the standpoint of biblical angelology, men are meant. 3. The title "sons of God" is not restricted in the Scriptures to angels. In biblical language the worshippers of a god are the sons or, as the word is frequently rendered, children of that god. If the whole nation is given to his worship, they are called the people of that god. The Israelites were the "sons of the living God" (Hos. i. 10), the "sons of Jehovah" (Deut. xiv. 1; xxxii. 19; Is. xliii. 6; xlv. 11), the "people of God" (with article, Judg. xx. 2). Israel was "his son" (Hos. xi. 1; Ex. iv. 22), Ephraim his "dear son" (Jer. xxxi. 20). The godly are "the generation of his children" (Ps. lxxiii. 15), while those who have dealt corruptly are "not his children" (Deut. xxxii. 4, 5). The Moabites were known as the people of the god Chemosh and as his sons and daughters (Num. xxi. 29 ; Jer. xlviii. 46). Under circumstances closely resembling those mentioned in the sixth chapter of Genesis, when Judah contracted heathen marriages, he was said to have married "the daughter of a strange god" (Mal. ii. 11). Even judges, because entrusted with the administration of divine law, are called "gods, the sons of the Most High" (Ps. lxxxii. 6). Sons of God was the proper title to apply to his worshippers among the antediluvians. 4. The title "sons of God"—a designation broad enough to include all godly men—is appropriate to the Sethites, who seem to be prominently before the mind of the writer ; for they were the worshippers of God. Despite the corruption into which they finally sank, they were distinguished as a godly race. The line of Seth began in a family which acknowledged the true God and recognized his goodness (iv. 25). In that line, in the next generation, God was worshipped in his character as Jehovah (iv. 26 and cp. v. 29). In that line was the Lamech who cherished a hope of redemption from the curse. In that line were Enoch and Noah, both of whom were conspicuous for their piety ; through the one God gave to the antediluvian world striking evidence of future life with God, and interposed to save the family of the other from the universal destruction. By right, therefore, the Sethites might be called the children or sons of God. 5. The use of the term "man" finds suitable explanation. It is not contrasted with God, but with the sons of God as a class, and means other men generally, as in Jer. xxxii. 20 and Is. xliii. 4, where in contrast with Israel it means men generally, people who are not of the chosen nation. God, it is said, did "set signs and wonders in the land of Egypt, even unto this day, both in Israel and among [other] men." After the same manner Gen. vi. 1-2 may be read : When man in

general began to multiply on the face of the ground and
daughters were born unto them, the sons of God saw the
daughters of men generally that they were fair; and they
married whomsoever they chose.   6. These unworthy
alliances are described in v. 3 as being the sin of man,
not of angels; and the offspring of the union are men,
not demigods, v. 4 (see below).   A period of one hundred
and twenty years is granted to man, not to angels, for
repentance; and the flood destroys sinful man, not fallen
angels.   7. The place occupied by this account in the
general narrative of Genesis suggests that the narrator
meant Sethites by the term " sons of God."   The writer
gave a history of the fall of man; he then recounted the
progress of evil, the downward course of sin, the origin
of two races or classes of people, their separate development and diverse moral tendencies; and finally he describes the intermarriage of the two peoples in order to
show how the godly were secularized and corrupted, and
to explain why there were not righteous men enough to
avert the deluge (cp. Gen. xviii. 20–33).

On broad scriptural grounds, therefore, and from the
details of the account and the place occupied by it in the
narrative, we conclude that by the sons of God the pious
race of the Sethites is meant.

The offspring of the mixed marriages were nephilim.
This word is rendered *gibbaraya'* by Onkelos, γίγαντες by
LXX, ἐπιπίπτοντες by Aquila, βίαιοι by Symmachus.
The etymology is doubtful.   Many derivations have
been proposed.   It has been traced, for example, to the
Assyrian *pâlu*, strong, mighty; and to the Hebrew
nāphal in the sense (1) of fallen, sinful beings, or (2) of
beings characterized by falling upon others, violent, or
(3) bastards, analogous to *nephel*, abortion, miscarriage.

The word occurs in but one other passage, namely in
the report of the ten faint-hearted spies concerning the

obstacles to the conquest of Canaan. They had seen the Nephilim, *i.e.*, Anakim, who were descended from the Nephilim; and in comparison with them the Israelitish explorers felt themselves grasshoppers (Num. xiii. 33). But these people were not giants in the sense usually associated with that term; they were not beings of super-human size and extraordinary power; they were not even exceptional; for it is expressly stated that there were other nations in Canaan "great and tall like the Ana-kim" (Deut. ii. 10, 20), and the spies reported that *all* the people of the land were men of stature (Num. xiii. 32). The Anakim were large, stalwart men, who had dis-tinguished themselves in war and whose invincibility had become proverbial (Deut. ix. 2). And the question remains unanswered whether the name Nephilim denotes largeness of frame or fierceness of disposition or lowness of birth.

In regard to the antediluvian Nephilim, a description of them is given in the verse in which they are named. They are not called men of stature. They are de-scribed as "mighty" men. The word employed is *gib-bôr*, which signifies a valiant man, or a warrior, or a hero. The mighty men whom David had are called *gib-bôrîm* (1 Chr. xi. 10, et seq.), but they were not giants. Of course the word might find fitting application to a gi-ant, but not in reference to his stature. The essential idea of the word is strength, not size. The Nephilim are further described as "the men of name" whose deeds of valor or violence got them "renown" (cp. Num. xvi. 2, 1 Chr. v. 24, and the deeds of David's mighty men, 1 Chr. xi. 22-24). Bodily strength and the disposition to exercise it in acts of violence would naturally appear in the offspring of the intermingling peoples; for it is a universally recognized fact that the engrafting of one race upon another not too different produces a more vig-orous type of men, and that marriage between the godly and the worldly results in a loss of spirituality and a lowering of the moral tone.

Only one other matter remains to be considered. Those who interpret the sons of God as angels (erroneously, we think) commonly discern a counterpart to the intermarriage of the sons of God with the daughters of men in certain tales of Grecian mythology. If the interpretation of the title " sons of God " which has been defended in the foregoing discussion be valid, there is no ground for such comparisons. But it may be well to waive the question of exegesis and to consider the alleged parallelism solely in the light of archæology.

Josephus, although he is of the number of those who identify the sons of God with the angels, sees nothing superhuman in their offspring. The latter were " despisers of all that was good, on account of the confidence they had in their own strength." And he adds : " The tradition is that these men did what resembled the acts of those whom the Grecians call giants." Have we then after all, as some have imagined, arrived at the myth of the giants ? Although Josephus, who is writing for Greek readers, points out only a resemblance between the actions, although the language of the Hebrew narrator does not imply beings of gigantic size, is the Hebrew record nevertheless nothing but a popular myth deprived of repugnant features and adjusted to the religion of Israel ? Is the narrative of the impious race and of their overthrow by the deluge at bottom the Greek story of the gigantic offspring of heaven and earth revolting against the gods and cast into the depths of the sea in punishment ? No ; for a part of the Hebrew narrative, it may be said at once, is not a myth ; the deluge is an historical fact. The sequel being history—and the narrative of the flood is evidently regarded as the sequel by the author of Genesis—the former narrative is not likely to have been a myth trimmed and adjusted to fit into the historical event. And as to the former part, the general Babylonian tradition, as will be shown in the chapter on the tower of Babel, did not look upon the persons destroyed by the flood as gigantic offspring of heaven and earth. A broader answer is given by Lenormant. "This myth," says Lenormant, speaking of the Greek story of the battle of the giants, "is exclusively naturalistic. These earth-born giants remain absolutely foreign to humanity, and continue to be solely the representatives of the forces of nature, no serious mythology ever having entertained the idea of associating the Gigantomachy with the cycle of traditions at the beginnings of human history" (Origines, p. 359 seq., Eng. Tr., 360).

Lenormant is more inclined to see the counterpart of the Hebrew narrative in the Greek stories of the heroes, "demigods born of the love of a god for a mortal woman or of a goddess for a mortal man." This is going far afield. The tales of the heroes are Greek, not Semitic. They do not accord with the spirit of early Babylonian mythology as known from the cuneiform inscriptions at present accessible and from accredited Babylonian historians who wrote their country's history in Greek. In Babylonian mythology, deities had spouses; but these consorts were divine and their offspring were gods. Ishtar endeavored to fascinate men, but human progeny did not result. Native Babylonian mythology has thus far failed to tell of a god entering into amorous union with a mortal woman and begetting "a mighty man, a man of renown" who was on earth in the days of old.[1] The present outlook is not favorable to the discovery of any such tale, much less of a host of such stories.

[1] The remarks of Professor Sayce in regard to the origin of Sargon of Agade have not been overlooked, but they are fiction of the Englishman's own devising (Hibbert Lectures, p. 27). The custom alluded to by Herodotus (i., 181 and 182) was, of course, a priestly arrangement.

XII

THE DELUGE

In the autumn of 1872 Mr. George Smith, while at work in the British Museum examining the clay tablets which had been exhumed at Nineveh, read, on a large fragment which he picked up, the words : "The mountain of Nizir stopped the ship. I sent forth a dove and it left. The dove went and turned, and a resting-place it did not find, and it returned." Perceiving at once the resemblance to the story of Noah, he began a search to find the remainder of the tale—a search which he prosecuted unweariedly for two years, not only among the thousands of broken tablets in the Museum, but also, through the liberality, first, of the proprietors of the Daily Telegraph, then of the trustees of the Museum, on the site of ancient Nineveh itself. Success crowned his efforts. Two years after the discovery of the first fragment he had secured portions of three distinct copies of the tale, had established an almost complete text, and had produced a fair translation. Since his lamented death several additional fragments have happily come to light to add to the completeness of the text and to assist in its interpretation.

The story, as the tablet on which it is recorded itself states, forms the eleventh episode of a national epic in celebration of the deeds of Izdubar, or, as there is some reason to pronounce the name, Gilgamesh, king of Erech. The great hero of the tale, having been smitten with a torturing disease on account of his insolence toward the gods, resolved to seek his ancestor, Tsitnapishtim, who had been translated to the gods, was then dwelling "at the mouth of the rivers," and had knowledge of life and death. After a long and toilsome journey he finally reached the desired locality, and Tsitnapishtim stood before him—a man of a generation long past, yet with the freshness and vigor of youth. Astonished Izdubar exclaimed : "How camest thou, Tsitnapishtim, to see life among the gods ? "

"I will open to you, Izdubar," replied Tsitnapishtim, "the concealed story, and also the oracle of the gods [with reference to the cure of your disease] will I declare. You know the city of Surippak, which stands on the Euphrates. That city was old when the gods who dwelt therein were moved at heart to bring about a flood-storm. God Anu was there among others, and Bel and Ninib. The god Ea, however, deliberated with them, and he revealed unto me their purpose [by means of a dream (l. 177)]. 'Man of Surippak, son of Ubaratutu,' said he, 'tear down the house, build a ship, despise property, and save life. Bring into the ship seed of life of every kind.' I paid attention and said to god Ea : 'O my lord, what thou hast commanded I will respect by carrying out.'

On the morrow [preparations were begun]. On the fifth day I laid the framework—140 cubits its height, 140 cubits its extent above. I divided its interior, I provided a rudder. Over the outside I poured three measures [sars] of bitumen and likewise over the inside. When the ship was completed I filled it with all that I possessed—with silver, gold, and seed of life of every kind. I took on board all my men-servants and maid-servants, the cattle and the beast of the field, and the artisans.

The sun-god set a time. 'When the sender of violent rain causes a heavy rain to pour down in the evening, enter into the ship and shut the door.' The set time came. He who sends violent rain caused a heavy rain to fall in the evening. The dawning of the day I feared, I trembled to behold the morning. I entered the ship, closed the door to shut it in, and committed the immense structure with its cargo to Puzur-Bel, the pilot.

As soon as the dawn appeared, a dark cloud ascended on the horizon. In the midst of it the storm-god rolled the thunder.

The gods Nebo and Marduk marched on before, went as guides over hill and dale; the mighty pest-god tore loose the ship, the god Ninib caused the streams to overflow their banks. The Anunnaki, spirits of the subterranean regions, lifted torches and made the land flicker by the light. The storm-god raised billows which reached to heaven. All light was turned to darkness. Man saw not his fellow, human beings were not discerned by those in heaven.

The gods also were terrified at the flood-storm, sought refuge, ascended to heaven, and crouched at the wall like a dog in his lair. Then the goddess Ishtar, like a woman in travail, cried out —she of beautiful voice called : 'Mankind which was is become mud, the very evil which I foretold in the presence of the gods and just as I foretold it to them. A storm for the annihilation of my people I declared it would be. I brought forth men, but to what purpose? Like fry of fish they fill the sea.' The gods over the spirits of the subterranean regions wept with her, sitting bowed in tears, their lips covered.

Six days and six nights [1] wind, flood-storm, and rain prevailed; on the seventh day the rain abated; the flood, the storm which had writhed like a woman in travail, rested; the sea withdrew to its bed, and the violent wind and the flood-storm ceased.

I looked on the sea, at the same time shouting; but all men were become mud. I opened a window; and, as the light fell upon my face, I shrank back and sat down weeping; over my cheeks the tears coursed. I had looked on every side—a wide expanse, sea.

A bit of land, however, rose to the height of twelve measures. To the country of Nitsir the ship took its course. A mountain of that land stranded the vessel and kept it from moving farther. On the first day and on the second day Mount Nitsir held the ship, on the third day and on the fourth day likewise, on the fifth and sixth days likewise. When the seventh day came I released a dove. The dove flew hither and thither; there was no resting-place, so it returned. Next I sent forth a swallow. The swallow also flew hither and thither and, as there was no resting place, re-

---

[1] Mentioning the nights as well as the days, as does the Hebrew narrative at the same point. For text see Expositor, September, 1888, pp. 236-37 ; Haupt, Beiträge, vol. i., 133; Jensen, Kosmologie, S. 430. Delitzsch, however, reads "six days and seven nights." His text thus contains a formula often found elsewhere, e.g., l. 188.

turned. Then I sent forth a raven. The raven flew away and, when it saw that the waters had fallen, it approached, alighting but not returning.[1]

I then sent forth [all the animals] to the four winds. I poured out a libation, I made an offering on the summit of the mountain. I set vessels by sevens, and underneath them spread sweet cane, cedar, and herbs. The gods smelled the savor and like flies gathered about the offerer.

When the goddess Ishtar arrived, she raised aloft the great ornament which the god of the sky had made at her request. 'By the ornament of my neck, never will I forget; I will think of these days and to eternity not forget them. Let all the gods come to the offering except Bel, for he inconsiderately caused the deluge and consigned my people to the judgment.' But Bel came also; and, when he saw the ship, was filled with wrath against the gods of the heavenly spirits. 'What soul has escaped?' he cried; 'not a man shall survive the judgment.' Then god Ninib opened his mouth and spake to the valorous Bel: 'Who else than god Ea has done this thing? Ea knows surely every exorcism.' Ea also opened his mouth and said to the valorous Bel: 'Thou, valorous chieftain of the gods, so utterly without reflection hast thou acted and caused the flood. On the sinner lay his sin, on the evil-doer his evil deeds. Desist [from wrath] that he be not cut off; be gracious also. Instead of causing a flood-storm send the lion and the hyena, famine and pestilence, and let them diminish men. And as for me, I did not reveal the purpose of the great gods; I sent Atrachasis a dream and he perceived the purpose of the gods.'

Then Bel became reasonable, went up into the ship, grasped my hand and led me up. He led up my wife also and made her kneel at my side. Then turning to us he placed himself between us and blessed us, saying: 'Heretofore Tsitnapishtim was a [mere] man; now let him and his wife be exalted to equality with the gods, and let him dwell afar off at the mouth of the rivers.' Thereupon he took me away and placed me afar off at the mouth of the rivers."[2]

---

[1] Or, the raven flew away and saw the abatement of the waters; [thereupon] he eats, alights carefully, but does not return.

[2] Such is essentially the cuneiform story. As here reproduced, it is slightly abridged; chiefly, however, by the omission of mutilated lines and of sentences whose translation is still uncertain.

8

Berosus also wrote an account of a flood. According to the extract which Eusebius made from the writings of Alexander Polyhistor, the statement of the Babylonian priest was to this effect:

" The tenth king of the Chaldeans was called Xisuthrus. In his day happened a great deluge. The god Chronos appeared to him in a dream and said that on the fifteenth day of the month Dæsius mankind would be destroyed by a flood; bade him therefore to engrave a history of the beginning, progress, and conclusion of all things and deposit it in Sippara, the city of the sun; to build a ship and embark with kith and kin; to convey on board, moreover, food and drink, and drive in animals both winged and four-footed; and having made all things ready, to sail away; if asked whither he is sailing, to say, 'To the gods; to pray for the good of mankind.'

He did not neglect the admonition, but built a vessel five stadia in length and two in breadth; put into it everything which had been ordered, and took on board his wife, his children, and his kinsfolk.

The flood having occurred, as soon as it abated Xisuthrus sent forth certain birds, but they, not finding food or any place where they might alight, returned to him to the vessel. After some days [1] Xisuthrus again dismissed the birds, and they now returned to the vessel with their feet muddy. Having sent them forth the third time, they came no more to the ship; whence he judged that land had appeared. He then pushed apart a portion of the covering [2] of the vessel, and, seeing that the ship was stranded on a mountain, left it with his wife and daughter and the pilot. He then worshipped on the earth; built an altar and sacrificed to the gods. Afterward, with those who had come out of the vessel with him, he disappeared.

When those with Xisuthrus did not return, they who had remained in the vessel quitted it and sought him, calling him by

---

[1] According to the extract which Eusebius takes from Abydenus, Berosus stated that the birds were sent forth on the third day after the cessation of the rain, and the second time after other three days.

[2] Properly, stitching; that which is stitched or united; hence a covering of cloth or skin as being stitched together, in distinction from a roof of planks. Cp. the Hebrew word in Gen. viii. 13, elsewhere used for the covering of skins wherewith the tabernacle was roofed.

name. Xisuthrus himself, indeed, appeared to them no more; but a voice came from the air admonishing them, as a thing necessary, to be religious; for on account of his piety he is on his way to dwell with the gods, and his wife and daughter and the pilot partake of the same honor. He told them, moreover, to return to Babylonia, and, as decreed, recover the writings from Sippara and give them to mankind; moreover, that where they now are is the land of Armenia. When they heard these words they offered sacrifices to the gods and journeyed on foot to Babylonia.

Of this ship, which was stranded in Armenia, a portion still remains in the Gordyæan Mountains of Armenia; from it people get bitumen, which they scratch off and use for averting evil."

The question of the relation of the subject-matter of the cuneiform tale to the story related by Berosus may be dismissed with a word. Beyond question the two accounts relate to the same event. Each tale originated (as will presently be proved) in Babylonia, each tells of a flood in Babylonia, each dates it in the earliest ages, each describes similar occurrences and in similar order, and in each the names of the hero and his father are etymologically the same; for Tsitnapishtim, it would appear from the tablet, was also called Atra-chasis, and as Smith pointed out, Xisuthrus is but the Grecized form of this cuneiform name, the component parts being transposed.[1] The father of Xisuthrus was Otiartes or Opartes, a name which corresponds to the cuneiform Ubaratutu.

But the relation of the cuneiform account to the story told by Berosus is of small interest compared with the question of the bearing of the Babylonian tradition on the criticism of the Hebrew narrative.

Preliminary to such an investigation it is necessary to know the exact relation between the Babylonian and Hebrew accounts. Is it quite certain that the flood re-

[1] TSBA., 1874, pp. 531-33; Haupt, Sintfluth, S. 23, Anm. 7; KAT²., S. 65 f.; Jensen, Kosmologie, S. 385 f.

ported by the Babylonians is the deluge recorded in
Genesis? What is the date and origin of the cuneiform
account? And what is the character of the cuneiform
story?

In regard to the identity of the flood described in the
two accounts, it is noticeable that the names of the leading persons are respectively different—so different as to
defy identification. The name Noah bears no outward
resemblance to Xisuthrus or Tsitnapishtim;[1] and Ubaratutu, or translated into Assyrian, Kidin-Marduk—*i. e.*,
Servant of god Marduk, none to Lamech. Nevertheless there is a striking coincidence; according to Berosus, Xisuthrus, the hero of the flood, was the tenth antediluvian king of Chaldea; and in the Bible Noah is the
tenth antediluvian patriarch.

The home of the hero may be the same according to
both accounts. The cuneiform tablet expressly states
that it was in Babylonia. Tsitnapishtim was a resident
of "Surippak, a city situated on the Euphrates," whose
patron deity was the Babylonian god Ea (II R. 60,
20 a, b). The same locality is indicated by Berosus,
who states that Xisuthrus was a Chaldean, the last of the
ten antediluvian kings of Chaldea, and the son of a king
from the city of Laranchae; that before entering the ark
he buried a written record of the world's history in the
city of Sippara in Babylonia; and that after the subsi-
dence of the waters, the ark having landed in Armenia,
he ordered his companions to return to Babylonia, which
they did, and again founded Babylon. In the Hebrew
account, as is well known, the residence of Noah at the
time of the flood is left indefinite. But since no migration of mankind from the neighborhood of the Tigris and
Euphrates (Gen. ii. 14) is recorded, the region watered

---

[1] Though Hommel endeavors to find support for reading Nuch-napishtim,
PSBA., vol. xv., 243

by these streams is suggested as still the place of his abode; likewise, if no stress be laid on possible changes in the face of the earth wrought by the flood, Noah's use of pitch in the construction of the ark indicates the bitumen pits of Babylonia. While therefore the Hebrew narrative makes no definite mention of Noah's home, its indirect references harmonize with the statements of the Babylonian story and admit the possibility that Babylonia was the locality whence Noah sailed.

Each of the three narratives contains a description of the vessel, the Hebrew and cuneiform records devoting large space thereto, whereas Berosus mentions but few features, and these for the most part incidentally. But no two of these accounts agree in their report of the dimensions of the ship. According to Berosus its length was more than three thousand feet (almost five times that of the Great Eastern), and its breadth more than twelve hundred. On the cuneiform tablet (l. 24) the length is given as 600 cubits, at least the traces which remain "lend themselves very well to the ideogram for . . . 600." The width and height were equal, each being 140 cubits.[1] The Hebrew, on the other hand, assigns but three hundred cubits to the length, and makes the width fifty and the height thirty cubits. In other words, if the same measure is to be understood by cubit, the ship of Tsitnapishtim was twice as long as the ark of Noah, more than twice as wide, and four times as high. But in whatever respects the cuneiform and Hebrew records may agree or disagree as to the dimensions of the vessel, their description of its origin and general structure seems to be similar. According to each, the ship was built by divine direction and according to a divinely furnished plan, was divided into compartments (l. 59), provided with a door (l. 84 and 89) and

---

[1] Haupt, PAOS., 1888, p. lxxxix.; Beiträge, vol. i., 124 ff.

window (l. 129), pitched within and without with bitumen
(l. 62, 63), and roofed over to protect it from the sea (l.
26; cp. Gen. viii. 13). And yet how different the vessels still! The ark (to judge from the name) was apparently a sort of raft, with sides and a covering which
was not wooden, and drifted about uncontrolled on the
waters; whereas the cuneiform narrative represents the
vessel as a "ship" which a pilot guided on its course.

In this vessel certain men and beasts were to find
safety. But here again the Hebrew and Babylonian accounts disagree. There is a marked difference in the
personnel. Noah went into the ark, and his sons and his
wife, and his sons' wives with him (Gen. vii. 7), "that is,
eight souls" (1 Pet. iii. 20); but Xisuthrus takes with
him, according to Berosus, not only his wife and children, including a daughter, but also his kith and kin
generally, and in addition a pilot; or, following the cuneiform report, his wife (of children not a word is said)
—his wife, his men-servants and maid-servants, the artisans and a pilot. And yet there is agreement between
the Babylonian and Hebrew traditions. In both the
hero was authorized to save not himself alone, but his
household as well, and he was commanded to take on
board with him living creatures of every sort, or, in the
phraseology of the inscription, "seed of life of every
kind" (l. 22 and 79), in order to "keep seed alive" on the
earth (Gen. vii. 3 and line 21).

The two accounts evidently differ furthermore as to the
duration of the flood; for while the Hebrew writer represents the storm as raging forty days, the cuneiform account allows but seven. Data for further comparison are
wanting.

The accounts also disagree as to the landing-place of
the vessel. The mountains of Ararat is the locality assigned by the Hebrew writer; a name that of old—cer-

tainly as far back as the period of the Assyrian Empire
—belonged to the plain of the Araxes. But the vessel
of Tsitnapishtim stranded on Mt. Nitsir. In the ninth
century before Christ a mountain was known to the Assyrians by this name. It stood east of the little Zab
River; 300 miles indeed south of Ararat, but yet in the
same mountainous region. Berosus fixes upon still a
third locality, one of the Gordyæan Mountains,[1] which lie
east of the Euphrates, near the river, almost equally distant from Ararat and Nitsir, but still in the same general
region of country.

But not to pursue the minute comparison of the two
narratives further, it will suffice to exhibit the common
tradition. By reason of man's wickedness,[2] God decreed
the destruction of all flesh, both man and beast, by a
flood. The divine purpose was revealed to one mortal,
the last of a line of ten worthies. This man was in-
structed to build a vessel of certain dimensions and according to a divinely given plan, to pitch it within and
without with bitumen, to stock it with food, to take into
it with him his wife and family, and likewise living creatures of every kind, not only domestic animals, but also
wild beasts and birds, in order " to keep seed alive upon
the face of the earth." The man did so. When the
advent of the deluge drew nigh, the man was divinely
warned now at length to gather his family and the animals together and to enter the ark, for the set time was at
hand. Again the man obeyed and entered the vessel.
The storm burst, the flood prevailed, and mankind was
destroyed. After some time the storm ceased, the waters
began to assuage, and the sea to withdraw to its bed.
The ship finally stranded on a mountain, and, round

[1] Now called the Djudi Mountains. According to Smith : " The present
tradition of the country places the mountain of the ark in the Jebel Djudi,
opposite Djezireh " (Assyrian Discoveries, p. 217).

[2] So apparently the Babylonian, l. 170.

about, the mountain tops became visible (order differs in the two accounts). After waiting some days the man, in order to inform himself of the state of the water, began to send forth at intervals various birds (of which both accounts mention the raven and the dove), and at length learned that the waters were abated. The inmates of the vessel, both man and beast, having gone forth, gratitude for deliverance was manifested by a thank-offering. And the Lord (or, in the Babylonian phraseology, the gods) smelled a sweet savor, and the Lord said : " I will not again curse the ground any more for man's sake, . . . neither shall all flesh be cut off any more by the waters of a flood." According to the Babylonian story, Ea pled with Bel in the assembly of the gods, saying : " [Hereafter] on the sinner lay his sin, on the evil-doer his evil deeds. . . . Instead of causing a flood, send the lion and the hyena, famine and pestilence, and let them diminish men."

Here, then, are the facts, and they admit of but one conclusion. Stated in a twofold manner this is :

1. The theme of the two accounts is the same ; the cuneiform and the Hebrew records describe the same event.

2. The Hebrew narrative, at least as a whole, has not been derived from the cuneiform ; the accounts are independent save in their common origin. For, be it observed, the Hebrew story is not simply the cuneiform tale stripped of its polytheism, but a variant version ; for even after the removal of the polytheistic elements the stories conflict. Many of the discrepancies have already been pointed out. It may be added that the accounts are notably at variance in the picturesque incident of the birds, as to their number, their kind, and the actions by which they furnished a clew to the condition of the waters.

Furthermore, no features of the Hebrew narrative were learned from the cuneiform tale in the time of the exile, and modified to harmonize with other Israelitish traditions; for, as will presently be shown, every incident of the Hebrew story was current in Israel before the exile. Antiquity belongs even to the variant portions. There certainly, therefore, lie before us two independently transmitted traditions of the same event.

With much less argumentation the date and origin of the cuneiform account may be established. It belongs, even in its present form, to a period earlier, and probably very much earlier, than the seventh century before Christ. The colophon impressed on the clay states that the tablet was the property of king Ashurbanipal (AL²., S. 109, Z. 295). This monarch reigned over Assyria from 668 to 626 before Christ. It is furthermore declared to be a copy of an older tablet (Z. 293); but the date of the original is not stated, and cannot be definitely determined. The great epic of Izdubar, of which the story of the deluge is an episode, originated in Babylonia; for the scenes are laid in that land. How early the tale existed there in the form in which it appears on the tablet remains uncertain. But the essentials of the tale were current centuries before Ashurbanipal's day. The appearance of Izdubar in engravings on gems and signet cylinders of the early Chaldean period, two or three thousand years before Christ, indicates this; and for the existence of the story of the deluge in special, testimony is afforded by an ancient name of the city of Surippak, where Tsitnapishtim, the hero of the flood and builder of the vessel, lived. It is called Ship-town (I R., 46, 1), a name which appears on monuments of the sixteenth century before Christ and earlier (Smith, TSBA., 1874, p. 589; Assyr. Disc., p. 212). As confirmatory testimony it may be mentioned that the god Ea, who revealed to Tsitnapishtim the coming flood, and ordered him to build the vessel, and protected him and his companions from the anger of Bel, was worshipped in this Ship-town as a patron deity of the city (II R. 60, 21).

The story of the flood, then, as told on the cuneiform tablet of the seventh century before Christ, was carried to Assyria from Babylonia, and in its essential features is traceable to the early Chaldean period.

It still remains to notice the character of the cuneiform account. While it has mythological features it is not a myth. A myth is an imaginary tale, which generally has some reference more or less remote to physical phenomena, but which has no other foundation in fact; the Babylonian story relates history.

For its historical character may be said : 1. Apart from its polytheism the Babylonian tale is credible. It describes a physical disturbance for which the alluvial plain of Babylonia is adapted (Süss, Die Sintfluth), and narrates an escape which in itself is probable. 2. The ancient Semitic peoples, both Hebrew and Babylonian, regarded the story of a flood, whereby all men except one family were destroyed, as historically true. They refer to it as a crisis in history. The Hebrews, and in portions of their writings which the divisive critics declare to be pre-exilic, describe it as a turning-point in human affairs, the beginning of a new race. Berosus devoted the second book of his Babylonian history to the ten antediluvian kings of the Chaldeans, considering the flood to mark the close of the first period of the history of mankind. Ashurbanipal refers to inscriptions " of the time before the flood " (Lehmann, Shamash-shumukin, Inscription 13, col. I., 18) ; and an Assyrian scribe, recording names of ancient kings, remarks concerning certain of them that they are "kings which were after the flood" (V R., 44, col. I., 20). 3. Confirmation of the historical character

of the Semitic tradition is afforded by the existence of
similar stories among other races; of special importance
being the Aryan tradition in India to the effect that a
man, saved from the waters of a world-wide deluge in a
vessel which finally landed on a northern mountain, became the progenitor of the new race of men. 4. It is
improbable that without such a catastrophe a tale should
arise of such extensive influence upon human thought.
For reasons such as these, it is almost universally recognized that a foundation of fact underlies the Semitic
story of the flood.

But while the cuneiform account treats of an historical
event, it yet elaborates facts into marvels, ceasing to be
history and becoming legend. Nevertheless the legendary element is small. Expunge the mythological language, and a tale remains in the main soberly told.

The results thus far yielded by the discussion are that
the cuneiform account is a legend; a legend which originated in Babylonia an unknown length of time before
the seventh century before Christ, and in its fundamental features goes back to hoary antiquity; a legend,
furthermore, which treats of the same event as the Hebrew record. It is now pertinent to inquire what light
this Babylonian story throws upon the related Hebrew
narrative.

The divisive critics affirm, as is well known, that two
accounts are interwoven in the Hebrew narrative of the
flood, of which one antedates and the other postdates
the exile. The critics essentially agree among themselves
as to which of the two component tales each several part
of the composite story belongs; and they agree also that
the existence of two component tales is established by
difference of style, repetitions, contradictions, anachro-
nisms. Before seeking light on this special question from
the cuneiform account, it is worth the effort to obtain a

clear view of the contents of the tradition as it circulated
in pre-exilic Israel. All critics agree that certain incidents related in the tradition of the flood were of old
current among the Hebrews. The Jehovist's version is
admittedly pre-exilic. The account of the ark's landing
and of the bow in the cloud are considered equally early
(Wellhausen, Proleg., S. 328–29). The only *incident* of
the Hebrew tale not yet accounted for is the introductory scene of the priestly post-exilic version, where the
command to build the ark is given, the reason for its construction stated, and the plan furnished. But this incident, in itself and apart from the literary form in which
it is narrated, was naturally a part of the current tale;
the command to build the ark logically belongs to a narrative of the flood, and would scarcely have been wanting in the Israelitish tradition. The opening sentence of
chapter seven, a portion of the "mutilated" version of
the Jehovist, implies that this incident was also in the
early tradition current in Israel; for it is improbable
that to the statement that the Lord determined to "destroy man from the face of the ground, . . . but Noah
found grace in the eyes of the Lord " (vi. 7, 8), there was
abruptly added : " And the Lord said unto Noah, 'Come,
thou, and all thy house into the ark.' " The wording of
this sentence seems to imply that the Jehovist's narrative in its complete form had previously mentioned a
command to build an ark, and contained some description of it. The evidence is strong that, while the Jehovist's account is admittedly pre-exilic, all the additional
incidents found in the priestly version were likewise
known in Israel before the exile, and probably included
in the Jehovist's narrative itself. The story of the flood
may have been repeated by the Israelites, as by people
of to-day, in a variety of forms and in diverse literary
style ; but however that may be, the Hebrew record, not

as parcelled out to different writers, but only in its present so-called composite form, tells *all the incidents of the flood as known of old in Israel.*

Furthermore, the Hebrew record in its present form corresponds, except in the one matter of the rainbow, incident by incident with the cuneiform account. The incidents of the Hebrew tale were known in pre-exilic times, and the cuneiform record dates in its present form from a period anterior to the seventh century. Here, then, is evidence that the tradition of the flood had a definite content before the separation of the two peoples; evidence also that the incidents of the Hebrew tale were not of Israelitish invention but belonged to the primitive tradition; evidence that the story, with its present material and present arrangement, is essentially the old tale as it came in with the Hebrew migration and as it lived from generation to generation in the mouth of the people.

It may be added that such details of description as the mention of bitumen, of periods of seven days, and of altar and sacrifice are also appropriate in a Babylonian tradition as early as the time of the Hebrew migration; that "the boundary line between clean and unclean animals is marked by nature," and their classification in a general way, according to this principle, is admitted by critics to have existed before Moses; that as for the olive, while it has never been known as a tree of the Babylonian plain, Strabo testified to its occurrence in Armenia; it is supposed to be indigenous in Northern India and other temperate Asiatic regions (Marsh, in Johnson's Cyclopædia); in its varieties it is now found "from the basin of the Mediterranean to . . . New Zealand;" and "the wild olive extends eastward to the Caspian, while, locally, it occurs in Afghanistan" (Encycl. Britan.). Not only, then, is there evidence that all the incidents of the flood found in the present Hebrew record were familiar to the Hebrew emigrants, but there is justification for the assumption that the salient features of the present description also existed in their day.

Notwithstanding the evidence that all the incidents of the Hebrew account were current of old in Israel and that even the details of description might appropriately appear in the narrative as early as the days of Moses, it is held that two accounts of the same event are interwoven in the present record and are distinguished from each other by style, by repetitions, and by contradictions. The modern theory of division is not restricted to the flood episode, but embraces a large portion of the Old Testament; it is only in regard to the narrative of the deluge, however, that a voice comes from remote antiquity to pronounce on the criteria and results of modern criticism. All the more attentively, therefore, let that voice be heard.

The divisive critics assert that the storm which produced the deluge is described twice in two successive verses of the seventh chapter. It is there written : "The same day were all the fountains of the great deep broken up, and the windows of heaven were opened ; and the rain was upon the earth forty days and forty nights." It is urged that here two literary styles are apparent : one vivid and poetical, the other the calm recital of prose ; that the descriptions are furthermore contradictory, the one representing the deluge as caused by rain only, the other by the outburst of subterranean waters also. An answer to this argument is not far to seek. No ordinary rain of forty days caused the flood ; the water poured from the clouds, streams overflowed their banks, the sea, disturbed perhaps by earthquakes, rolled its waves upon the land. To tell this tale it does not suffice to speak of a rain. Adequate description requires the writer to say, using oriental imagery, that the windows of heaven were opened and the fountains of the great deep broken up. To tell how long the storm lasted, speaking no longer as a spectator, but as a statistician, he adds : "And the storm was upon the earth forty days and forty nights."

The cuneiform tale confirms this view, utterly depriving the critical argument of force. Describing the raging of the storm as a spectator, the Babylonian writer is picturesque and vivid. "As soon as the dawn appeared, a dark cloud ascended on the horizon. In the midst of it the storm-god rolled the thunder. The gods Nebo and Marduk marched on before, went as guides over hill and dale ; the mighty pest-god tore loose the ship ; the god Ninib caused the streams to overflow their banks ; the Anunnaki lifted torches and made the land to flicker ; the storm-god raised billows which reached to heaven. All light was turned to darkness ; man saw not his fellow, human beings were not discerned by those in heaven." This is the language of enthusiasm and poetry. But when the narrator comes to state how long the storm lasted, he adopts a very different style of speech, saying : "Six days and six nights wind, storm, and rain prevailed ; on the seventh day the rain abated, the storm which had struggled like a woman in travail, rested ; the sea withdrew to its bed, the violent wind and the flood-storm ceased."

The cuneiform account does not disprove the theory that two narratives are combined in the Hebrew record of the flood, but it shows that a method employed to distinguish the documents is precarious. In the only case where the method can be tested, it fails. Difference of style is not an infallible evidence of diversity of document.

It is contended, however, that throughout the Hebrew account two contradictory conceptions of the flood are represented. Again the cuneiform tale offers a suggestive parallel. In the Hebrew record, the first mention of the deluge is in the portion ascribed to the priestly writer; God forewarns Noah that a destructive flood of waters is impending, but reveals not whether by rain or by tidal wave or by both. In the cuneiform tale, the approaching destruction of man is foretold, and Tsitnapishtim bidden to *build a boat*. The catastrophe accordingly would be wrought by a flood of *water ;* but whether in the form of rain from heaven, or freshet from the northern mountains, or inflowing sea is not disclosed. But when the set time draws nigh, the prophecy becomes definite and foretells rain. God warns Noah to enter the ark— the other writer, according to the divisive critics, relates this—saying : " Yet seven days and I will cause it to rain upon the earth." Likewise the cuneiform account (a change of authorship is not thought necessary), as the time approaches, becomes definite. " When the sender of violent rain causes rain to pour down in the evening, enter into the boat." When the storm breaks both writers, as already shown, become vivid in language, using familiar imagery. Finally in retrospect, according to the Hebrew record, God promises not to again cut off all flesh by the waters of a flood ; while, according to the inscription, the god Ea pleads that another such storm may not again destroy mankind. Surely, in view of the absolute similarity which obtains between the cuneiform inscription and the Hebrew record, in their description of the flood, no critic is authorized to say that the language of the Hebrew record is *on this subject* contradictory, and indicative of two writers with different conceptions.

The testimony of the cuneiform tale is, indeed, insufficient to disprove the theory that the narrative of the flood is a compilation out of different documents. But the argument for two documents which is based on difference of style is proven to be of doubtful value; for in one important test case it is found on evidence from antiquity to be invalid and untrue. And the claim that the extracts from the reputed documents are contradictory and therefore unhistorical is proven false at every point where it can be tested by antiquity. The charge of discrepancy has been recklessly made and is groundless.

This ancient testimony in regard to the Hebrew record of the flood has wider reach than that narrative. It has important bearing upon fundamental principles of the divisive criticism, and it calls in question the correctness of the application of these principles in the past.

The exegetical importance of the Babylonian tale is small, so far as it concerns words and phrases, its legendary character, as well as the tendency sometimes apparent in it to embellishment, rendering it an untrustworthy guide. Occasionally, however, it is suggestive, as when it fixes upon a "mountain of the land Nitsir," and not upon "the mountains of Ararat," as the landing-place of the ark; for the mountain known in Ashurnatsirpal's day as Nitsir stood hard by the district called Urtû. Originally Hebrew and Babylonian accounts were one, and of course indicated the same locality; the question is justly raised whether the like-sounding words Urartu (Ararat) and Urtû (the t in each is teth) have not afterward become confounded.

The fact, however, now clearly apparent that the Hebrew narrative is a tradition transmitted through the fathers is of vast exegetical importance; for it materially aids in determining the scope of thought. The narrative originated in the account of eye-witnesses and has been handed down as other traditions have been. Its lan-

guage is, of course, to be understood in the sense it bore
to men centuries before the days of Moses; and it must
not for one moment be forgotten that the men of that age
had a totally different conception of the world from what
we have, and meant a totally different thing by the expression "the whole world" from what we would mean.
What do these men of olden time, who were eye-witnesses
of the catastrophe and whose description of the event
was determined by their conception of the world, say of
the extent of the flood?   Those who escaped the destruction told their children after them that God revealed the
coming of this flood to a certain man and warned him to
provide a vessel for the saving of his house, directing him
to take every kind of land animals with him into the vessel for the preservation of brute life, announcing that the
waters were sent to blot out man from under heaven because of his abounding iniquity, and that beasts and rep-
tiles were to be involved in the destruction (vi. 19, P, and
vii. 4, J.).   The survivors related also that the man who
had been forewarned heeded the admonition and built the
ark.   The flood came.   During its supremacy, according
to the testimony of these eye-witnesses, all the high mountains that were under the whole heaven—*i.e.*, which were
within man's changing horizon—were covered and that
all flesh wherein was the breath of life, man and cattle
and creeping thing, perished, and that they alone who
were in the ark escaped.   They bore witness to what they
had seen.   Their later observation and the experience of
their descendants who transmitted the tradition confirmed
the impression first made of the destruction of life, for
as they journeyed they found the earth empty.   The
deluge had accomplished the purpose of God.

No testimony for or against a universal deluge is contained in the tradition, either in its Babylonian or Hebrew
transmission, unless it be involved in the announced pur-

pose of God to destroy man whom he had created from
the face of the ground, both man and beast and creeping
thing and fowl of the air.[1] Even this announcement is
not testimony to a universal deluge, unless animals were
distributed over all parts of the globe. Moreover the
language which is used to announce the divine purpose
must not be interpreted as meaning more than the sense
which it conveyed to the people to whom it was addressed.
It must be interpreted also in the light of the probable meaning which Noah attached to the command to
him to take every sort of animals with him into the ark
and especially to the command to take all food that is
eaten; for he certainly did not attempt to penetrate
distant unexplored regions of the earth in order to discover unknown animals and secure for them their own
peculiar and indispensable food. Finally the language
must be interpreted without violence to the require-
ments of passages like Joel iii. 1; John xii. 32; Dan.
vi. 25.

To the discussion of the Semitic tradition of the flood,
which has occupied the preceding pages, the chronology
of the Hebrew account is appended as the concluding
paragraph. The scheme is worthy of consideration because of its uniform adherence to the data of the Hebrew
text, because of its constant employment of the method
used by the Hebrew writer, and because of the peculiar
interlocking of its results.

It appears from verses three and four of the eighth
chapter compared with the seventh chapter and eleventh
verse that the months are reckoned at thirty days each,
and that the number of days which measure an interval
of time are obtained by subtracting the earlier terminal
date from the later or, *vice versa*, the later date is found

---

[1] Gen. vi. 7; doubtless equivalent to "man and with him beast, etc." Compare further vi. 13, 17; vii. 4; viii. 21; ix. 10, 15.

by adding the given days to the earlier date. Employing this method strictly, the following chronology results:

vii. 4 and 10.	COMMAND TO BEGIN EMBARKING THE ANIMALS,	2 mo.	10th day.
vii. 11.	ENTRANCE OF NOAH INTO THE ARK, and, later in the day, bursting of the storm,	2 mo	17th day.
vii. 12.	Rain was upon the earth 40 days and 40 nights, so that the		
	RAIN CEASED toward evening	3 mo.	27th day.
vii. 24.	The waters prevailed on the earth		
viii. 3ᵇ.	150 days, so that the		
viii. 4.	ARK STRANDED	7 mo.	17th day.
	The waters decreased continually until the		
viii. 5.	TOPS OF THE MOUNTAINS WERE SEEN	10 mo.	1st day.
viii. 6.	After seeing the mountain tops, Noah waited 40 days; expecting that, as the rain had fallen 40 days, the waters would perhaps abate from the ground in 40 days; and then (or on the following day) the		
	RAVEN RELEASED, which returned not,	11 mo.	11th (or 12th) day.
	After 7 days (cp. "yet other," v. 10) a		
viii. 8.	DOVE RELEASED, which returned,	11 mo.	18th (or 19th) day.
	After yet other 7 days, the		
viii. 10.	DOVE RELEASED, which returned with an olive leaf. So Noah knew that the waters were abated from off the earth.	11 mo.	25th (or 26th) day.
	After yet other 7 days, a third time the		
viii. 12.	DOVE RELEASED, which did not return, since by this time food and shelter were to be found outside of the ark,	12 mo.	2d (or 3d) day.
	Notwithstanding these favorable indications, Noah did not leave the ark, but waited for God's command. After nearly a month's waiting, on New Year's day,		
viii. 13ᵇ.	NOAH REMOVED THE COVERING OF THE		
viii. 13ᵃ.	ARK, and saw that the waters were dried up and the face of the ground was dried,	1 mo.	1st day.

But Noah still awaited God's bid-
ding, and eight weeks later, the earth
being dry, God gave the
viii. 14, 15.   COMMAND TO GO FORTH FROM THE ARK,   2 mo. 27th day.

The results of the chronology are that the first day after
the terrific storm was the forty-ninth from the command
to embark the animals and the forty-second from the
entrance of Noah into the ark. The first day that dawned
bright with peace and with divine favor was a recurring
seventh day. The ark stranded in the middle of the
week, a date without significance at the time; but the
tops of the mountains were seen on the first day of the
tenth month, which was a recurring first day. The new
world, like the old, began on the first day of a week.
Noah released the birds successively either on the recurring sixth day, in expectancy of the morrow, or on
the recurring seventh day itself. Noah removed the covering of the ark on the first day of the first month. It
was New Year's day, but the expectancy of divine favor
may have been awakened by the fact that it was the recurring seventh day. But while his hopes were not dis-
appointed, for the waters were dried, he yet awaits God's
command. Eight weeks later, on the recurring seventh
day, Noah is bidden to disembark. It was a day of divine favor and a day of release to the captive.[1]

Some of these recollections are preserved in the other
transmissions. Josephus, in his slightly variant version,
also measures the period from the mission of the birds
to the release of the animals from the ark by sevens,
though he does it in a different manner from the biblical
narrator. The cuneiform account preserves the memo-
ries that the premonitory storm burst in the evening,
that the tempest ceased on the seventh day, that a period

[1] In both narratives out of which the Hebrew record is said to be composed,
the week plays a part, whether the two documents be combined or separated.
In J., vii., 4 and 10, viii., 6-12 ; in P., vii., 11, compared with viii., 5, 13ᵃ, 14.

equal to the duration of the rain was allowed to elapse after the stranding of the ark before essay was made with the birds to ascertain whether the waters had disappeared, that the dove was sent forth on a seventh day, and probably that the exit from the ark took place on a seventh day ; though, as to the last matter, the writer transmits the tradition of his own people ambiguously and leaves his statement in such a form that it might be understood as meaning that the several missions of the birds and the disembarking of the inmates of the ark took place within the same twenty-four hours.

XIII

THE MIGHTY HUNTER

THE tenth chapter of Genesis is a table of the nations of the ancient world. It is a bare catalogue of peoples and communities in the form of a genealogy; based in part on political and geographical relations, but chiefly on the kinship of the included nations.

In the midst of this barren enumeration of names and affinities, a person full of life and action and human passion appears, who would be a notable figure in the picture of any age, but who stands out in sharper relief against the unembellished background. Nimrod was more than a mere link in the genealogical chain, serving only to mediate the succession; he made history. "He began to be a mighty one in the earth. He was a mighty hunter before the Lord. And the beginning of his kingdom was Babel and Erech and Accad and Calneh in the land of Shinar."

A counterpart to Nimrod exists in the person of the great hero of early Babylonian story, who is commonly known as Izdubar, or, as there is reason to pronounce the name, Gilgamesh. The history of the two celebrities is strikingly similar. Both were kings who ruled in the land of Shinar and numbered Erech among their cities. Both lived after the flood and traced their descent from the hero of that event. Both were noted hunters; Izdubar being a slayer of wild beasts, whose encounters with animals, not less than his exploits in war, were embodied in a poem and formed a favorite subject for engraver and

IZDUBAR.

Mural sculpture of Sargon's Palace.   Height of figure, thirteen feet and a half.

sculptor. But while the comparison of Izdubar and Nimrod is interesting, their identity has not been proven.[1]

In view of the possibility of such identity, however, the person of Izdubar requires a brief notice. The story

[1] For nearly ten years the champion of the identification of Izdubar with Nimrod has been Professor Hommel. His argument has been presented before the Society of Biblical Archaeology and is published in its Proceedings, vol. viii., 119; xv., 291; xvi., 13. Stated briefly, the argument is that the patron deity of Izdubar was Lugal-turda; and that the wife of this god was Nin-gul, a goddess who is declared to be identical with the goddess Nin-gal, "*gul* being only a somewhat later pronunciation of *gal*, great:" but the goddess Nin-gal was the wife of the moon-god Sin; accordingly the moon-god Sin is one and the same deity with Lugal-turda, the god of Izdubar. Again, the end of two lines of a bilingual text remains which read

. . . . Sin lord of x-y-bar-ra
. . . . Sin lord of god namra tsit.

On another tablet the similar statement is found,

Sin lord of god x-y-bar-ra
Sin lord of namra tsit.

Hommel affirms that the character indicated by x, which is a single horizontal wedge, has the value *gi* which belongs to the upright wedge. The character which is represented by y was frequently used by the Assyrians as ideogram for their word *ishdu*, "foundation." Here then is a rebus: the Ninevite scribes have playfully employed the Assyrian equivalent of a sign when writing a Babylonian text; and they intended the upper line to be rendered " Sin, lord of Gi-ishdu-bar-ra." But further, the moon-god Sin was, as already argued, the god of Izdubar, or Gishdubar, as Hommel would read the name; and the lord of Gi-ishdu-bar-ra is, according to the bilingual inscriptions just quoted, the lord of namra tsit: from which it follows that Izdubar or Gishdubar equals Namratsit or Nimrod. The argument rests, in the first place, on the assumption that Nin-gal and Nin-gul are identical, for which there is not the shadow of proof. It also requires the second sign in the name Izdubar to be pronounced *du*, as indeed is currently done; though, so far as appears, the dental is not properly *daleth*, but *teth* or *tau*. As to the word or phrase namratsit, it is found elsewhere with the context (Sin) [Sha] namrat tsitka (Strassm Alph. Verzeich., 8063), means "bright as to rising" (Delitzsch), and, according to Jensen, is an epithet of the new moon. The god Sin is the lord whose rising is bright, or the god Sin is lord of the new moon. It may be added that the identification proposed by Hommel is rejected by Delitzsch and Jensen.

A question distinct from this is interwoven by Professor Hommel in his later articles. Izdubar equals Gilgamesh, according to the fragment of a tablet discovered by Mr. Pinches. Gilgamish (with mish for mesh), Hommel thinks, " was originally Gibil-gamish." In VR. 30, 6f, is found the divine name Gi(sh)-bil-ga-mish. To this god or deified man people in remote antiquity

of which he is the hero is an elaborate legend. The tale
is divided into twelve cantos, whose incidents have been
thought to follow the course of the sun through the zodiac, though Izdubar himself is unquestionably distinguished from the sun. Izdubar's "mother was the goddess Aruru" (Jeremias, Izdubar-Nimrod, S. 6). His
own name is preceded by the determinative for god,
which probably indicates that he was regarded as a
deity; and a prayer is extant which was offered to him
for health. These things, however, must not obscure the
fact that Izdubar is distinctly a man and that back of
the innumerable legendary details of the story there is a
"historical background." He is indeed said to have
been begotten or built by the goddess Aruru; but this
expression must be understood in the same sense as
the similar one is when it is said that Nebuchadnezzar
was begotten by the god Marduk, and Ashurbanipal
by Ashur and Sin, who created or built each of these
kings " in the womb of his mother " (India House, col.
i., 23-24; V. R., i., 3-5). Izdubar has the divine determinative before his name, and was in a sense deified;
but in this respect he does not differ from other early
Babylonian kings whose historical existence is established. Sargon of Agade, for example, and his son Naram-Sin appear with the determinative for god before
their names; and Tsitnapishtim, the hero of the flood,

ascribed the building of Erech's ancient wall, ancient even in those early days.
Erech was the capital of Izdubar's kingdom. These passages Hommel contends
must govern the reading and restoration of the mutilated text quoted by Jensen (Kosmologie, S. 386). Accordingly instead of the pronunciation and restoration Gish-tu-bar-[r]a — Gish-ti-i[-bir ? ?], Hommel reads Gish-du-bar-[r]a
— Gi-bil-g[a-mish].

 The latter argument contains an element of plausibility. If correct, it
proves that the name which George Smith provisionally read Izdubar represents the name Gil- or Gibilgamish, and that in the hoary past he was regarded
as builder of an ancient wall of Erech. It does not, however, identify Izdubar with Nimrod. The question of identity remains precisely where it was
before.

is, in one instance, deified in the same manner.[1] Like a
man, Izdubar made a thank-offering to heaven for vic-
tory; like a man, he was a worshipper of the gods, his
especial protector being the patron deity of the town
Marad. He was a descendant of the hero of the flood,
an ancestor who is expressly called a man and referred
to as a mortal. Izdubar himself is repeatedly denomi-
nated a man; and he was smitten with disease, was subject to death, obtained but lost an herb which had virtue to rejuvenate him. He was a noted hunter, and a
warrior who by a deed of valor freed Babylonia from
Elamite rule, and in return was rewarded with the throne
of Erech. Though prayer is addressed to "god Izdubar," it is to him as judge who acts "like a god," and as
one to whom "the sun-god has intrusted a sceptre and
judicial decision." Prayer was made to him, but it
would seem to have been done after his apotheosis; just
as it is offered to his ancestor Tsitnapishtim, who had
been translated to dwell with the gods (IV R. 59, col.
iv., 8). As to the setting of the story in which Izdubar
is the hero, it is historical; the eleventh canto is the history of the flood, decked out though it is with legendary
embellishments; and the third, fourth, and fifth cantos,
which form the body of the tale and contain the essential parts of the career of Izdubar, relate to the successful revolt of the people of the plain against their
Elamite oppressors and the subsequent foundation of a
Babylonian kingdom. The available facts thus indicate
that Izdubar was a man.

[1] Sargon with determinative PSBA., vi., 12, without vi. 11, III R. 4, No. 7,
1. IV R. 34, Obv. 1 ; Naram-Sin with TSBA., v. 442, without I R. 3, No. vii.,
IV R. 34, Rev. 11 ; Tsitnapishtim with IV R. 59, col. iv., 8. Compare further,
but with caution, Dungi with I R. 2, No. ii., 1 and 4, without 2 and 3, with
both personal and divine determinative I R. 68, col. i., 10 (which of course
makes it probable that the name is compound, having as its first constituent
god Bau); Gamil-Sin with IV R. 35, No. 4 ; Amar-Sin with I R. 3, xii., and
5, xix ; Ishmi-Dagan with I R. 2, v. and vi.; Rim-Sin with I R. 3, x.; Nur-
Ramman with I R. 2, iv.

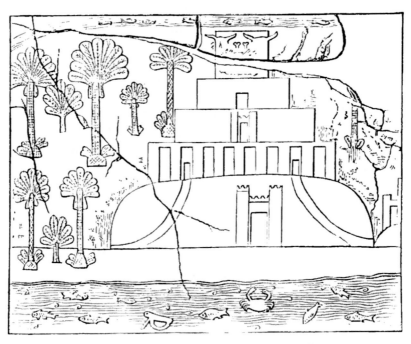

ANCIENT BABYLONIAN TOWER IN STAGES.

XIV

THE TOWER OF BABEL

THE translation of a cuneiform text was published by
Smith in his Chaldean Account of Genesis, and afterwards
by Boscawen in the fifth volume of the Transactions of
the Society of Biblical Archaeology under the title of the
" legend of the tower of Babel." Although this title was
bestowed upon it, the inscription was not put forward by
either of these writers with confidence as a tradition akin
to the Hebrew narrative, and its right to the title has
been questioned by other scholars (Delitzsch, Bezold).
It is, however, still quoted as authority by Professor
Sayce in his Hibbert Lectures. He says: The text
"gives us, as I believe, the Babylonian version of the
building of the tower of Babel" (p. 406).

The tablet is badly mutilated. Only two lines are in-
tact, it would seem, and some are so far gone as to leave
but a single word; and a gap exists in the middle of the
story where the tablet has been broken away entirely.
Smith's belief that the text might have reference to the
incident at Babel was based on a conjectural version.
He ventured to translate thus: "He confounded their
speech. Their strong place (tower) all the day they
founded; to their strong place in the night entirely he
made an end. In his anger also word thus he poured
out: to scatter abroad he set his face" (cp. lines 7 and
16–19 below). Smith's version is now known to be in-
correct; and the text has no obvious reference to the
building of the tower of Babel or any other tower, and

no likeness to the narrative in Genesis. The resemblance
to the Hebrew account, which Professor Sayce discovers,
appears only when the lacunæ have been filled by his fertile imagination.

The fragments of the inscription are exhibited in the
following translation in the position which they occupy
on the tablet, in order that the reader may judge for
himself what the subject of the story is. In lack of a
context to determine the meaning of ambiguous grammatical forms, preference is given in doubtful cases to
the rendering adopted by Professor Sayce.

```
"  . . . . . . .   his . . .   his heart was hostile
  . . . . . . . . the father of all the gods they hated
  . . . . . . . .   his . . .   his heart was hostile
  . . . . . . . . Babylon he was hurrying to seize¹
  . . . . . . and great were mingling² the mound
  . . . . . . . . Babylon he was hurrying to seize¹
  . . . . . . . and great were mingling² the mound
God Lugal-du-azaga³ made lamentation (?)  . . . .
In front of him god Anu . . . . . . . . . . . .
To god Anu his father . . . . . . . . . . . . .
Because his heart  . . . . . . . . . . . . . .
Who was bearer of intelligence (?)  . . . . . . .
In those days . . . . . . . . . . . . . . . .
        ?       ?     . . . . . . . . . . . .
Goddess Damkina . . . . . . . . . . . . . . . .
  . . . their [feminine] . . all the days he troubled (?)
During their [feminine] lamentation    in      bed
  . . . . . . . . . . . . . he did not end distress
In    his    wrath    he    overthrows   secret   counsel
  . . . his . . .  mingle designs (?) his face he set
  . . gave a command (? ?) changed was their [masc.] plan."
```

Although no record of the attempted building of the
tower at Babel and the confusion of tongues has been

¹ The translation "to seize," which is given by Professor Sayce, is considered by the writer to be impossible.

² The word is rather to be rendered "destroyed."

³ The name means "king of the chamber of destiny."

found in cuneiform literature, a tradition of such an event was current outside of Israel, and was ascribed by the transmitters of it to Babylonia. Whatever its origin, it is worthy of notice. In his History of the Chaldeans, Abydenus quoting Berosus, as is commonly believed, says:

"There are some who say that the men who first arose [or, following a different text, the first of the earth-born], having become puffed up by reason of their strength and stature, and having despised the gods in the imagination of being better than they, undertook a lofty tower where Babylon now is. It was already near heaven when the winds came to the aid of the gods and overthrew the work upon the builders. The ruins of it are said to be Babylon. Hitherto men had been of one tongue, but now discordant speech was sent upon them from the gods; war also was begun between Chronos and Titan."[1]

Alexander Polyhistor quotes the Sibyl, whoever that may have been,[2] as saying:

"When all men spoke the same language, some of them built an exceeding high tower in order to ascend into heaven. God, however, having made winds to blow, thwarted them and gave to each a language of his own; wherefore the city was called Babylon. After the flood, further, Titan and Prometheus were born; at that time also Chronos was warred upon by Titan."[3]

[1] Clause beginning "war also" is not quoted by Cyril of Alexandria in his citation of Abydenus.

[2] The Sibyls were ten in number. "The first was from the Persians, and of her Nicanor made mention, who wrote the exploits of Alexander of Macedon. . . . The fifth was of Erythræa, whom Apollodorus of Erythræa affirms to have been his own country-woman and that she foretold to the Greeks, when they were setting out for Ilium, both that Troy was doomed to destruction and that Homer would write falsehoods. . . . She inserted her true name in her verse, and predicted that she would be called Erythræan, though she was born at Babylon. . . . She is regarded among the others as more celebrated and noble." (Lactantius, Divinæ institutiones, I., vi.).

[3] The last clause is not quoted by Syncellus in his extract from Alexander Polyhistor, but is included in the citation as contained in the Armenian Chronicle of Eusebius. The entire reference to Titan, Prometheus, and

Why should Chronos-Saturn, Titan, and Prometheus be mentioned in the same context with the tower at Babel? Are these elements native or do they betray the assimilation of the Babylonian tradition to the Greek myths?[1] If they are native elements, what Babylonian names are concealed behind the Greek forms? When Berosus speaks of Chronos-Saturn, he means the Babylonian deity Ea, as appears on comparing his account of the flood with the cuneiform version; and in the passages cited relating to the tower of Babel, where Chronos is mentioned the Armenian Chronicle quite properly understands the god of that name to be intended and renders it accordingly. But who are meant by Titan and Prometheus? They "were born after the flood," and between one of them and Chronos war raged.

These various questions are difficult to answer; but whatever reply may be made to them, the kinship of the tradition, so far as it relates to the tower and its builders, with the Hebrew narrative is unmistakable. That it is an independent tradition is seen in its statement that the tower was destroyed, and that the winds were employed in the work of destruction. Josephus validly cites it from the mouth of the Sibyl as a voice outside of Israel speaking of the event.

Chronos is lacking, perhaps because irrelevant, in the quotation of the Sibyl by Josephus (Antiq., I., iv., 3) and by Cyril of Alexandria (contra Julianum, lib. I.).

[1] According to the story as told by the Latin poet Ennius (239-169 B.C.), Titan was a god, son of Cœlus and Vesta, and elder brother to Saturn. Although the senior, he yielded the kingdom to Saturn on condition that he raised no male children. Saturn violated the agreement; and Titan, taking with him his sons who are called Titans, made war upon his false brother and imprisoned him. The truth of this history is taught by the Erythræan Sibyl, who speaks almost the same things (Lactantius, Divinæ institutiones, I., xiv.). This is a different story from the tale which recounts how Zeus hurled the Titans, the twelve children of Ouranos and Gaia, out of heaven into nether darkness. See also Moses Chorenensis, I., c. 5, and Lenormant's remarks, Bérose, p. 416 seq.

A summary of the intervening events between the flood and the erection of the tower at Babel is furnished by a curious passage in Artapanus and a fragment from Hestiæus, which it will be seen may be put forward with considerable confidence as representing Babylonian traditions. They supplement the Babylonian narrative of history subsequent to the deluge, and serve for comparison with the corresponding Hebrew account. Artapanus is speaking of Abraham and remarks that "in certain anonymous writings we find Abraham tracing his lineage to the giants who dwelt in Babylonia and who on account of impiety were destroyed by the gods. One of them, Bel, having escaped death, settled in Babylon, and having built a tower lived in it, which was accordingly called Bel from Bel the builder" (Eusebius, Præp. evang., ix., 420). The passage is full of errors. Bel was a god, not as in the tale one of the giants; the tower he occupied in Babylon was not erected by himself, but was built for his earthly abode by his worshippers and was the chief temple of the city. But in spite of these misconceptions, the story is based on genuine Babylonian traditions: an impious race was destroyed by the gods; one notable person escaped; Babylon was settled by the saved and a tower erected there, which was occupied by Bel. This odd distortion of Babylonian tradition is elucidated by a fragment of Hestiæus. He says : "Those of the priests who were saved took the sacred vessels of the warlike Zeus [i.e., Bel][1] and came into Senaar of Babylonia" (Josephus, Antiq., I., iv., 3 ; Euse-

---

[1] Zeus=Bel (Berosus Βῆλος "ὃν Δία μεθερμηνεύουσι," and Herodotus, I., 181, 183) = Marduk. Ἐννάλιος Ζεύς recalls Quradu Bel, "the valorous Bel" who figures in the story of the deluge (l. 14, 164, etc.), one of the triad Anu, Bel, Ea. The brief passage from Hestiæus is an interesting example of the blending of the triad with Bel-Marduk, the chief deity of the Babylonians, the establishment of whose worship in Babylonia is here attributed to the survivors of the flood.

bius, Præp. evang., xiv., 416). Bel is not regarded by Hestiæus as a mortal who alone of his wicked fellows escaped the anger of the gods, but is recognized as himself a deity. It is some of his worshippers who were delivered from the destruction; those of the priests who were saved brought his sacred vessels to the land of Shinar. The confused story is falling into its proper components. The Babylonian tradition of the flood appears : the wicked race of men was destroyed by the gods; one favored individual with his retainers was saved ; these survivors, exhorted by Xisuthrus-Noah their leader, returned to Babylonia, and founded the city and erected the tower of Babel.

But were the builders of the tower giants ? Abydenus merely says that they were vain of their strength and size, but Artapanus and Eupolemus [1] expressly call them giants, and Cyril of Alexandria uses the same term in his rendering of Abydenus. But whatever idea may have gained currency in later times and in regions remote from Babylonia, the Semitic tradition as it flowed through native channels gives no intimation that the men engaged in these enterprises and involved in these punishments were, in any true sense, gigantic. The offspring of the mixed marriages are described by the Hebrew writer as men of might and renown ; but the generations that proceeded from them, the race destroyed by the deluge, the persons saved, their descendants who undertook to build the tower and were scattered throughout

---

[1] " Eupolemus in his book on the Jews of Assyria [Chaldea] says first the city of Babylon was founded by those saved from the flood (they were giants) : further, they built the tower which is mentioned in history ; but this having been overthrown by the intervention of God, the giants were scattered throughout the whole world " (Eusebius, Præp. evang., ix., 418). Eupolemus is identified, rightly or wrongly, with the Jewish envoy of the same name who was sent to Rome by Judas Maccabæus about 161 B.C. (Præp. evang., ix., 17). Artapanus is supposed to have been an Alexandrian Jew living about a century before Christ.

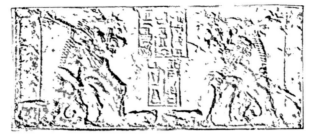

IZDUBAR AND THE LION.

IZDUBAR AND EABANI IN CONFLICT WITH THE BULL AND THE LION.

IZDUBAR AND THE BULL.   EABANI AND THE LION.

IZDUBAR AND THE LION.

the earth in consequence, are not distinguished as men
of unusual size or strength. On the contrary a man of
might like Nimrod is as worthy of note after the flood as
before it. And the same is true of the description of
these men of early times which is given by the native
cuneiform documents. It is not yet so complete as the
Hebrew record, but so far as it goes its testimony is to
the same effect as the Hebrew. The race destroyed by
the flood, Tsitnapishtim and his companions who were
saved, their descendants including even Izdubar, are not
mentioned as though gigantic. Izdubar indeed has colossal proportions, many times larger than a lion, in the
sculpture which adorned the walls of Sargon's palace, and
occasionally elsewhere.[1] A man who performed mighty
deeds of valor and was "perfect in strength," was, of
course, powerfully built and would naturally be represented as large. But even Izdubar, "the perfect in
strength" is commonly delineated no larger than human
in comparison with the beasts which he slays. The reference to the strength and size of the builders by Abydenus
and some other transmitters of the tradition may be due
to the influence of Greek myths and to the habit of regarding the men of the post-Trojan period as the degenerate sons of stalwart ancestors, not like Tydides who
"grasped in his hand a stone—a mighty deed—such as
two men, as men now are, would not avail to lift" (Iliad,
v. 302); or else, these Greek transmitters mean by their
words what Josephus means when he says that the builders of the tower imagined their prosperity to be derived
from their own power, and adds that Nimrod their leader
was "a bold man and of great strength of hand."

---

[1] The size is largely determined by artistic considerations. In the mural
sculptures of Sargon's palace, Izdubar is standing beside colossal bulls and
approximates them in size. Where the dado is narrower, the figures of Sargon and his attendants are frequently over nine feet in height.

10

The account of the tower of Babel which has been transmitted by the Hebrews is a tradition. This fact must govern interpretation. The survivors of the flood and their descendants, as they journeyed up and down in the earth, found no traces of other men. The eight persons who were saved in the ark and their posterity constituted the world. Few in numbers at first, they increased, until eventually, long after the time contemplated in the tradition of the tower of Babel, they had spread over Western Asia and into Europe and Africa, as their ancient tabulator could exhibit. This body of people in its earlier period is what the tradition means by the world (v. 1). For a considerable time after the flood "the whole earth was of one speech and one language." But it came to pass that man at length journeyed from, or in, the East, moving either *en masse* or in a body sufficiently large to be called "all the earth," and settled in the land of Shinar.[1] Doubtless they spoke the language they had used in the country from which they migrated; and if they left some of their brethren in the old home, there was still unity of speech among the now *disjecta membra.* This body of men, moreover, whether coextensive with all the descendants of Noah or only with that large part of his posterity which through dim recollection or intercourse remained in the knowledge of the settlers in Babylonia, constituted henceforth "the world" in the mind of the transmitters of the tradition of the tower of Babel. This is a necessary restriction of the term; by "world" man meant and could only mean the inhabitants of the earth

---

[1] The Babylonian tradition of the flood as transmitted by Berosus appears to bring back immediately to Babylonia those survivors of the catastrophe who did not disappear with Xisuthrus to the realms of the gods. The Hebrew narrative leaves it indefinite whether Noah remained in the neighborhood of the mountain where the ark stranded or returned to the locality of his former abode. The tradition of the tower of Babel has in view descendants of Noah remoter than sons, and people numerous enough to be called the whole world.

so far as their existence fell within his knowledge. This usage of the word is not only necessary, it is historical.

The settlers in Babylonia said: " Let us make brick and build us a city, and a tower whose top may reach unto heaven, and let us make us a name, lest we be scattered abroad upon the face of the whole earth." The end they had in view was to prevent their dispersion. The words suggest that men had already begun to scatter, an occurrence which of itself would give rise to dialect in speech; or, if the separation of men and the division of language had not commenced, the words indicate that signs of the weakening of social bonds were visible. A city and a tower would counteract the tendency to disperse, would secure permanence of abode, would form a centre about which they could cluster and to which in their wanderings their minds would revert, would awaken pride in their bosoms at the thought of personal connection with a great and prosperous community. The motive was one of vainglory, but God thwarted their purpose. An act of judgment—we know not what—resulted in confusion of their speech, so that they did not understand one another. The consequence was division of the populace, cessation of the public works, dissolution of the nation, and eventual emigration to all parts of the known world.

It should be observed that the change of speech is not asserted to have been sudden, though it may have been; much less is it asserted that all differences observable in languages the world over, or even those characteristic differences which distinguish the great families of language, owe their origin to the confusion at Babel. The event at Babel must not be minimized, neither must it be exaggerated.

History tells of migrations of people from Babylonia, which originated or aggravated dialectic differences in language. In most of these cases undoubtedly the sep-

aration of the people permitted the development of pe-
culiarities in speech and not *vice versa*, as in the tradition of the tower of Babel, did the difference of language
lead to the migration. Whether any of these movements
of population, therefore, are alluded to in the text cannot at present be determined.

The meaning of the name Babel. The native forms of
the name are *babilu* and *kadingira*, which signify "gate
of God." The designation is very ancient, earlier than
the days of Abraham. It is an appropriate name for a
city where God executed judgment; for the gate of a
town was a customary place of judgment. In stating
why the city was called Babel, the Hebrew writer is not
giving an etymology of the name, but relating the occasion which gave rise to it; and in doing so he adopts a
favorite method, employed in both the Old and the New
Testaments, and out of the words at his disposal to express confusion selected that one which approximated
Babel in sound. Men called its name Babel because
there the Lord did *balal* the speech of all the earth, and
thence did scatter them abroad upon the face of all the
earth.